Human Rights

A Practical Guide for Managers

Peter Villiers

KOGAN
PAGE

To Carolyn

The masculine pronoun has been used throughout this book. This stems from a desire to avoid ugly and cumbersome language, and no discrimination, prejudice or bias is intended.

First published in 2001

Apart from any fair dealing for the purposes of research or private study, or criticism or review, as permitted under the Copyright, Designs and Patents Act 1988, this publication may only be reproduced, stored or transmitted, in any form or by any means, with the prior permission in writing of the publishers, or in the case of reprographic reproduction in accordance with the terms and licences issued by the CLA. Enquiries concerning reproduction outside these terms should be sent to the publishers at the undermentioned addresses:

Kogan Page Limited
120 Pentonville Road
London N1 9JN
UK

Kogan Page US
22 Broad Street
Milford CT 06460
USA

© Peter Villiers, 2001

The right of Peter Villiers to be identified as the author of this work has been asserted by him in accordance with the Copyright, Designs and Patents Act 1988.

British Library Cataloguing in Publication Data
A CIP record for this book is available from the British Library.
ISBN 0 7494 3630 1

Typeset by Saxon Graphics Ltd, Derby
Printed and bound in Great Britain by Biddles Ltd, Guildford and King's Lynn
www.biddles.co.uk

Contents

Preface

This book is intended as a practical guide for managers to a subject that crosses the boundaries of law, management and political theory. We believe that human rights are essentially simple concepts, if at times their application can lead to complex arguments; and that they are not the exclusive possession of professional lawyers. We all have human rights, and we should all be able to understand what they mean and argue the extent of their application.

While professional lawyers, whether generalists or human rights specialists, may be helpful and indeed on occasion necessary in this process, the field is not theirs alone. If this little book helps its readers to an informed and strategic viewpoint, then it will have achieved its objective. If it corrects misunderstandings along the way, then so much the better.

We support the Human Rights Act and believe that it is a beneficial development. The Act will create a quiet revolution, which it behoves managers in all sectors to take part in rather than to resist or ignore. Managers do have rights for themselves, as well as a responsibility to uphold them for others. Welcome to reading and using this guide, for both purposes.

Human Rights, A Practical Guide for Managers sets out to demystify human rights and to enable its readers to share and use a common language. The only cases referred to are those that are necessary to explore the general implications of human rights, and there is no attempt to explore every twist and turn of the plot. As the proverb says, a little knowledge can be a dangerous thing, and this book will not qualify anyone as an all-purpose expert in human rights. It will, however, give readers the opportunity to reach a position where they can debate human rights issues, in broad terms, on a common level with professional specialists. They will then be in a better position to decide for themselves which issues are important, and which arguments are false, incomplete, one-sided, or misleading, and they will be able to take matters forward as they wish to do.

The contents of the book are self-explanatory by chapter heading, and follow a logical sequence. We believe that perhaps its most useful ingredient is the list of questions and practical case studies, to be found at the end of each chapter, in which readers are encouraged to apply themselves to practical problems. We have attempted to make these case studies both realistic and challenging, and must point out that the comments attached to them are not intended as definitive solutions but a stimulus to further thought, reading or research. We suggest that group discussion of some of these dilemmas, however arranged, will be beneficial to the thoughtful manager.

May we finish by saying that human rights form an organic whole as well as a set of discrete rights and freedoms, and that we have approached them in that light. Some rights are so closely related that it has not always been either practical or desirable to pry them apart, and we have not attempted to do so. In the same vein, Article 14 prohibits any discrimination in regard to any of the rights and freedoms set forth in the Convention. It is thus a right of general (although not unlimited) application, and we have applied it in any case study where it appeared to fit.

Acknowledgements

I am obliged to the many lawyers who have enlightened my ignorance and provided guidance on human rights from many angles, including Alex Carroll, Parosha Chandran, Ralph Crawshaw, Conor Gearty, Karim Khan, Laurence Lustgarten, Sara Mansoori, Lars Mosesson, Peter Noorlander, Quincy Whitaker and my brother Kit Villiers. They have been most helpful in offering me the benefit of their disinterested advice. If I did not always take it, I remain extremely grateful for their friendly and unpretentious erudition.

As always, I am indebted to my professional colleagues at the Police Staff College, with whom I have often debated human rights issues, and who have increased my understanding of both law and human nature.

Finally, may I acknowledge the help of my publishers, and point out that any errors in the text, whether of fact or judgement, remain my own.

1

The origins of human rights

Human rights are abstract concepts with practical consequences. They are rights that international institutions such as
the United Nations have declared that all human beings
possess, simply by virtue of being human. Although we cannot
see, touch, feel or smell these rights, we know that they exist; we
know them to be important; and we know that they should be
recognized everywhere.

Human rights have three characteristics:

1. They are *inherent*. (We are born with them.)

2. They are *universal*. (We are all born with them.)

3. They are *inalienable*. (We cannot give them away, either for
   ourselves or for other people. We cannot, for example, voluntarily sell ourselves into slavery in order to be fed.)

Rights need to be taken seriously.

In a world that officially and universally subscribes to the
importance of human rights, we must recognize that this state of

affairs was not always the case. We must also recognize that a true alternative is not just a casual disregard for human rights, so that what is upheld in theory is simply neglected in practice.

Neglect is not an alternative theory; and the categorical opposite of the recognition of human rights is despotism. The absolute despot believes that might is right, and that his subjects are there purely for his benefit. Whether they be called slaves or not, their position is in fact one of slavery, in that any benefits which they obtain are offered purely at the discretion of their master and may be withdrawn at any time, to be replaced by the presumably more usual fare of suffering and misery. The slave, by definition, and in distinction to the servant or serf, has no rights. However well he may be treated on a day-to-day basis, that depends upon the pragmatism of his master, and not on any contract between the two. This is recognized in the Universal Declaration of Human Rights, which places an absolute ban on slavery.

Why should the despot be the master, and the slave, the slave? Why, indeed? Some despots have found a convenient philosophical niche in the notion of divine right, or its oriental variations – the idea that God has ordained them to be king, and that no subject has the right to question any of their actions. They may, like the Japanese or Inca emperors, claim descent from the sun itself: but not all absolutists make such claims.

The despot may recognize that he has a duty to care for the welfare of his subjects. The Inca empire, for example, was founded on the premise that the Emperor would provide food, order and festivities for his people, and was an interesting example of a socialist ethic imposed from above. While in this context we may therefore refer to the obligations or responsibilities of the ruler, we cannot talk of rights.

Thomas Hobbes, the great English philosopher, lived through the English civil war and was profoundly affected by its horrors. It was he who described the natural life of man, in one of the most telling phrases of political philosophy, as nasty, poor, solitary, brutish and short. Hobbes believed that anarchy was the worst of evils, to be avoided at almost any price. A strong state was necessary to avoid anarchy, and a strong state required an absolute ruler. The social contract was then the theory in fashion to explain the origin and necessity of the state and the disparity of power between ruler and ruled.

In Hobbes' version the ruler should be given absolute power, because only thus could he preserve the integrity of the state from which all other benefits flowed. The ruler is there for the benefit of the ruled, and this theory is thus an advance on divine right, which could be used to justify anything on the basis that the ruler has knowledge or wisdom that cannot be shared with or even understood by the subject. The subject, in Hobbes' world, may disagree with the particular action of the ruler: but at least he is aware that the ruler is there to prevent anarchy, and the broad sweep of his actions must lead in that direction.

In the last century the world has seen such rulers as Lenin, Stalin, Mao Tse-tung and Pol Pot claim absolute power to rule on behalf of others, and then set out to destroy both their happiness and their lives with an utter disregard for any notion of the most basic rights, in the name of some future goal clear only to the ruler. We cannot plight our troth with absolutism, no matter what its ideology; and there is no such thing as an enlightened despot. We need to control our leaders and limit their power, by the ballot box and other means.

Democracy, however, is not enough: for a formal democracy can still ride roughshod over the interests and needs of minorities. Democracy in its literal sense means simply rule by the people, and that can be interpreted to mean that all the state need do is to find out and follow the will of the majority.

But the will of the majority, in John Stuart Mill's telling phrase, can simply become the tyranny of the majority. Mill condemned what he saw as the tyranny of the majority over artistic freedom, as for example in the practice of state censorship of the arts. But, as he also recognized, the tyranny of the majority may in fact be used to suppress the freedom of the minority in any area.

On what principle, then, can and should the will of the majority be restricted?

JOHN STUART MILL ON LIBERTY

John Stuart Mill (1806–1873) was an English philosopher and East India Company administrator whose most influential work was probably his relatively short essay, *On Liberty* (Lerner, 1961) first published in 1859. In a nutshell, Mill believed that the (mature) individual was the best guardian of his own interests, and should be left free to act as he chose, provided that his acts did not directly harm others. We quote:

> *The only purpose for which power can be rightfully exercised over any member of a civilized community, against his will, is to prevent harm to others. His own good, either physical or moral, is not a sufficient warrant… Over himself, over his own mind and body, the individual is sovereign.*

Mill set out to distinguish between vice and folly. He believed that the state was entitled to act so as to prevent or at least control the former, but must allow its citizens the opportunity to be foolish. Why? Pragmatically, we might argue that it is easier for the majority to agree on what is a vice than what is a folly: but that was not Mill's point. He saw liberty both as a virtue in itself and as an essential need in a mature society of autonomous human beings, in which the state and its institutions were free to attempt to influence the citizenry, but not to control their behaviour.

Liberalism in practice

We may see examples of the application of Mill's principle all around us today. Consider the sale of tobacco. Young children, by definition, are not free and autonomous adults. Even a liberal-minded follower of John Stuart Mill would generally accept that the state has a duty to protect children from the consequences of their folly until they are of a proper age to choose for themselves. Hence, children are not allowed to buy cigarettes. (We might dispute the effectiveness of the ban, but that is another matter.)

Adults, however, are allowed to buy tobacco, even though the state is very much aware of the positive connection between smoking and cancer. Thus, children are stopped from smoking, whereas adults are allowed to smoke but warned of its consequences. Why does the state simply not ban tobacco outright?

In terms of the prevailing social philosophy, this is because it recognizes the consumption of tobacco as a folly, but not a vice, and because the damage caused is primarily self-regarding. We could suggest other and less philosophical reasons why the government licenses rather than bans the sale of tobacco, but that is the liberal one; and it is only one example among many of the attempt to apply John Stuart Mill's 'very simple principle' in everyday life.

Reflections on John Stuart Mill's importance

John Stuart Mill's influence on political and social life has been profound, and it would be hard to name a British philosopher, with the exception of his near-contemporary Jeremy Bentham, whose views have had a greater general effect. We live in a Millian world, at least as far as our freedom of expression is concerned, and so far as we are prepared to reconcile the potentially antagonistic concepts of the freedom of the press and its private ownership. State censorship is not a popular activity, outside the pressing social needs of wartime, and Mill's dictum that we should be free to do what does not harm others has been used as a general principle in a whole range of issues where some citizens, whether inside or outside parliament, have sought to restrain or curtail the liberty of expression of others.

Mill's very simple principle is not usually in itself the solution to a dilemma; but it helps to clarify the underlying issues. It is the outstanding principle to which we can appeal when we wish to restrain the authority of the state, where the state's declared intention is to protect the interests of the individual against himself. But it does not cover all situations, and it was a far from adequate principle to protect the citizen against the ravages of the state in the century that followed Mill's.

Reflection

Where do you think that Mill's very simple principle might be most difficult to apply?

What connection can you draw between this principle and the notion of human rights?

HUMAN RIGHTS IN THE CONTEMPORARY WORLD: WORLD WAR II AND THE CONSTRUCTION OF A NEW WORLD ORDER

World War II can be seen through many perspectives. For some of its participants it was seen as a conflict between good and evil. The crimes against humanity that the Axis powers committed – the tortures, the arbitrary executions, the mass extermination programmes against innocent peoples who had been declared racially inferior – were the evidence of their evil. It was particularly shocking to the victors that those who had transgressed the most were those who had the furthest to fall. The Nazi killing machine was the product not of some medieval tyranny, but of what would beforehand have been described as a highly advanced civilization. With the end of the war good had triumphed over evil, at least for the time being. But that evil could re-emerge, and if a highly developed society such as Germany could succumb to it in the past, was anywhere safe in the future? International political action was needed to prevent tyranny from re-emerging and destroying the lives of ordinary people – in any state, and whatever its association with democracy.

The creation of the United Nations

The United Nations (UN) was set up in New York in 1946 on two levels: the General Assembly and the Security Council. It needed an ideology, or at least a doctrine. What did the UN stand for? What values did it exist to promote? It could hardly refer simply to the virtues of bourgeois or liberal democracy, since that pattern of political and social organization was limited to the industrial democracies of the West. What values could all or most of the nations of the world, whether capitalist or communist, Christian or Buddhist, colonial or colonized, formally recognize?

The Universal Declaration of Human Rights (1948)

The UN produced its Universal Declaration of Human Rights (UDHR) as the doctrine, or at least the aspiration, towards which all nations could subscribe. We will not list the whole of this declaration, which contains 30 articles, and is easily to be found elsewhere. Here is its preamble:

Whereas *recognition of the inherent dignity and of the equal and inalienable rights of all members of the human family is the foundation of freedom, justice and peace in the world,*

Whereas *disregard and contempt for human rights have resulted in barbarous acts which have outraged the conscience of mankind, and the advent of a world in which human beings shall enjoy freedom of speech and belief and freedom from fear and want has been proclaimed as the highest aspiration of the common people,*

Whereas *it is essential, if man is not to be compelled to give recourse, as a last resort, to rebellion against tyranny and oppression, that human rights should be protected by the rule of law,*

Whereas *it is essential to promote the development of friendly relations between nations,*

Whereas *the people of the United Nations have in the Charter reaffirmed their faith in fundamental human rights, in the dignity and worth of the human person and in the equal rights of men and women and have determined to promote social progress and better standards of life in larger freedom,*

Whereas *Member States have pledged themselves to achieve, in cooperation with the United Nations, the promotion of universal respect for and observance of human rights and fundamental freedoms,*

Whereas *a common understanding of these rights and freedoms is of the greatest importance for the full realization of this pledge,*

Now, therefore,

The General Assembly

Proclaims *this Universal Declaration of Human Rights as a common standard of achievement for all people and all nations, to the end that every individual and every organ of society, keeping this Declaration constantly in mind, shall strive by teaching and education to promote respect for these rights and freedoms and by progressive measures, national and international, to secure their universal and effective recognition and observance, both among the peoples of Member States themselves and among the peoples of territories under their jurisdiction.*

These are inspiring sentiments. Are they enough? Do they, together with the rights that follow them, have the power to change behaviour, or are they condemned to remain as ideals towards which we may aspire, but never actually achieve?

We need to see the 1948 declaration as fulfilling several purposes. It is clearly a statement of aspiration, but it is also more. In 1948, many of the world's countries were incapable of putting into practice the measures and mechanisms that would have allowed their people to have achieved these rights, no matter how much they wished to do so.

Some of the aspirations of the 1948 declaration, however, were more easily capable of being made a reality than others, at least in terms of financial cost. Now as then, it may prove impossible for a relatively poor country to feed, clothe, educate and maintain the good health of its population, even supposing that its government accepts that it has a direct responsibility for those actions.

A fair trial, however, is another matter. It need not be any more expensive than an unfair trial. Indeed, in the long run it is likely to be economically much more beneficial. What are we really saying? That there are some rights which the state can set out to provide quite simply and cheaply, and without any overt ideological commitment. They are usually referred to as political, individual, or even negative rights, whereas the rest are usually known as social and economic rights. The UDHR contains both, and that is both its strength and its weakness.

Ubi Remedium, Ibi Ius

Whatever the contents of a particular declaration of rights, there is always one question that has to be asked: where is the remedy? Hence the pithy Roman proverb: 'Where there is a remedy, there is a right' and not, to complete our brief venture into Latin, vice versa.

Where is the remedy for UDHR? That is a difficult question. Strictly speaking, there is no remedy, at least for the citizen of the state, which has promised to uphold these rights for his benefit and then fails to do so. International pressure may be applied to a state that fails to maintain these rights for a number of its citizens or subjects. That pressure may become very strong indeed. It ranges from ritual condemnation, to suspension or expulsion from the UN itself, to sanctions, economic or otherwise, or even war. However, it is not the same as an individual remedy for the individual citizen: and moral persuasion or even economic pressure is not the same as a court of law.

WHICH RIGHTS APPLY IN EUROPE?

For practical purposes, the human rights that we possess as Europeans, or as subjects within the jurisdiction of European states, are those that the Council of Europe has declared that it is prepared to protect. Other rights may exist in the abstract, as it were; but if we have no legal or constitutional means for claiming their protection, then no matter how important or desirable they may sound, they are of little practical use.

The Council of Europe

In 1945 Europe had been shattered by the rise of totalitarianism and its bloody culmination in World War II, and post-war leaders were determined to prevent the repetition of the abuses that had occurred.

The Council of Europe was created in May 1949 to promote a free, democratic and peaceful Europe by upholding three things: pluralist democracy, human rights, and the rule of law.

Like the three legs of a milking-stool, all three are both interdependent and indispensable. Even a democratic state may violate human rights, and the will of the majority needs to be fettered by a legally enforceable respect for the rights of the minority.

Originally consisting of 10 countries, the Council now contains 41 member states, and is still expanding. The Council of Europe, which is entirely separate from the European Community and the European Court of Justice in Luxembourg, consists of various representative institutions. Here we are solely concerned with the jewel in its crown: the European Convention on Human Rights (ECHR) and its mechanism for enforcement, the European Court of Human Rights (ECtHR).

The European Convention on Human Rights (1950)

The new convention, which was drafted in 1950 and came into effect in 1953, was based upon the UDHR of 1948. It concentrated upon what are traditionally described as political and constitutional rights, and left social and economic rights to be addressed by other means. The main rights it covers are as follows:

▊ The right to life.

▊ Liberty and security of the person.

▊ The right to a fair trial in civil and criminal matters.

▊ Respect for private and family life, home and correspondence.

▊ The right to freedom of thought, conscience and religion.

▊ Freedom of expression, association and peaceful assembly.

▊ The right to marry and found a family.

The following are expressly prohibited:

▊ torture and inhuman or degrading treatment;

▊ slavery and forced labour;

▊ retroactive criminal laws.

Later protocols

Protocols have been added to the ECHR, substantially increasing its range. They include, for example, the right to freedom of movement and the right to the peaceful enjoyment of one's possessions. Not all of these protocols have been signed or ratified by the UK. However, it is wise to be aware of their existence.

Enforcement

Until 1998 the task of protecting human rights was shared by the Commission and the Court of Human Rights, and the Committee of Ministers, the decision-making body of the Council of Europe, composed of the foreign ministers of member states or their deputies. (It is important to know that both Commission and Court previously offered judgements, as both are quoted in the literature.)

As from November 1998 a new, full-time European Court of Human Rights replaced the part-time monitoring institutions. The Committee of Ministers no longer has jurisdiction to decide on the merits of cases. Right of appeal to Strasbourg remains available only when domestic remedies have been exhausted.

In general, the ECHR and its mechanism for enforcement provide an arena for issues to be raised that would not otherwise obtain a hearing. It forces states to account for their actions or inactions, and internationalizes what might otherwise remain as domestic disputes. It is, as its founders described it, the conscience of Europe.

QUESTIONS

1. What do you understand by rights, and how would you distinguish between rights, privileges and obligations?

2. Why, in your opinion, does the Council of Europe link together human rights, pluralist democracy and the rule of law as the three essential foundation stones of a mature and successful democratic society?

3. How would you define the tyranny of the majority? What examples can you give of its possible operation in the society around you?

4. In a functioning democracy that allows for the expression of conflicting views in its representative assembly, the press and other outlets, and which does not practise censorship of contrary opinion to the prevailing view, why should the people have the right to protest?

5. Under what conditions do you believe that the state could be justified in censuring or prohibiting the free expression of opinion, or the free exchange of information?

These questions raise very broad issues about the nature of a liberal democracy. Some comments – but _not_ the right answers – will be found below, to which you may choose to refer after addressing these topics for yourself. In a liberal democracy, the debate is of the same order of importance as the outcome.

COMMENTARY

1. _What do you understand by rights, and how would you distinguish between rights, privileges and obligations?_

   There are various ways in which rights can be defined or understood, and your understanding may be as valid as any other. The text refers to rights as being innate, universal and inalienable, but that still does not tell us what they are. We will describe them as moral possessions that are part of what defines us as human beings. Rights, unlike privileges, do not need to be earned and cannot be taken away. In theory, we may have rights without obligations, but not vice versa. (We cannot have obligations without rights, since we cannot give away our rights.)

   In our view, however, rights and responsibilities – a word in this context meaning much the same as obligations – go together. My rights are someone else's responsibilities. We cannot enjoy our own rights without accepting responsibility for respecting the rights of others. A society that guaranteed rights without responsibilities would be a contradiction in terms.

2. _Why, in your opinion, does the Council of Europe link together human rights, pluralist democracy and the rule of law as the three essential foundation stones of a mature and successful democratic society?_

   In our opinion all three items are necessary for a democratic society, and each depends on the other two. Pluralist democracy ensures both that the will of the majority is heard strongly and that minority opinions are also expressed and play their part in influencing public policy. The will of the people must be able to be expressed in more than one way, and the existence of formal representative democracy does not guarantee pluralism. A healthy, functioning democracy has a representative assembly, an aspiration to universal literacy, a free press, a tradition of free speech, a respect for peaceful protest, and a number of ways in which citizens can express and lobby for their views, whether individually or collectively. Pressure groups are a sign of a healthy pluralist democracy, as is the emergence and development of non-governmental organizations, which may be as large and influential as Oxfam, or simply a gathering of two or three people.

Respect for human rights means that minority issues and concerns cannot be disregarded under some crude majoritarian formula, and that even democracy itself is tempered by a respect for fundamental principles. For example, even if an overwhelming majority voted for a particular policy, it might still be in breach of human rights. Moreover, there is an international dimension to human rights, so that the policy of a particular state, even if the will of the people of that country, may still contradict human rights as internationally agreed.

The rule of law means, in our view, at least four things:

- The law must be known, clear and comprehensive.

- The legal process must always be followed.

- No one is above the law.

- Those who are responsible for turning policy into practice do not bend or break the rules in doing so.

The police officer, for example, who decides that it is more important to protect society from dangerous people than to ensure that all suspects receive a fair trial, is not applying the rule of law. Nor is the politician who does not declare his assets as required, or who seeks to reward or promote a friend by using his connections and bypassing the official system.

The rule of law applies to everyone and everything, and no one and nothing is above it. Only if this principle is applied can we be sure that the will of the majority, with respect for minority rights, is consistently and fairly applied. Human rights must be respected in practice and not just in theory.

3. *How would you define the tyranny of the majority? What examples can you give of its possible operation in the society around you?*

John Stuart Mill referred to the tyranny of the majority in the sense of an oppressive dictatorship over taste and opinion, whether enforced by law or public opinion. He believed that if the will of the majority were to prevail in all areas, then we should live in a very dull and conformist society, in which individuality would be crushed. Not only would this damage our social and political life, but our economic vitality would also suffer. Sir Karl Popper took this argument forward in his great work, *The Open Society and its Enemies* (Magee, 1973) in which the author points out that it is not a coincidence that the most economically successful nations in the world are democracies, and that dictatorships are inherently unstable. Systems, policies and practices improve by debate and opposition, and conformity leads to stagnation.

There is no official formula to define the tyranny of the majority. We should refer to where the majority rides roughshod over minority opinion, in any sphere.

It is not necessarily, in our view, an example of tyranny if the majority legislates in favour of something to which the minority objects, or even objects strongly. Some people will always be opposed to taxation, but that does not in itself make compulsory taxation immoral. However, compulsory taxation, like any other scheme intended to affect everyone, should be the product of a democratic decision-making process in which minorities and objectors can make their views felt.

What of examples? In our view the banning of foxhunting represents the tyranny of the majority, and an infringement of human rights to boot. Readers may not agree with this, and will have many examples of their own!

4. *In a functioning democracy that allows for the expression of conflicting views in its representative assembly, the press and other outlets, and which does not practise censorship of contrary opinion to the prevailing view, why should the people have the right to protest?*

The Council of Europe sees the right to peaceful protest as the cornerstone of a democratic society, and believes that this right must be preserved alongside formal representative democracy. There are a number of reasons as to why this view should be upheld, some idealistic and others rather more pragmatic. Let us list a number of them as they occur to us, and see if your reasons are there:

- No representative democracy can perfectly express the will of the people. All representative systems are a compromise. Therefore, protest is necessary in order to express views that might not otherwise be heard.

- Peaceful protest is part of *pluralist* democracy. In other words, it give citizens more than one way to express their views and it allows for the spontaneous, direct and unregulated expression of opinion. Like the verdict of the jury, it is the expression of the people rather than someone else speaking on their behalf.

- Peaceful protest may be intended more for its symbolic effect than to achieve an immediate outcome. Even if protest does not lead to a change of policy, people will have had their say.

- Peaceful protest is a safety valve for the expression of intense feelings that might otherwise be expressed destructively. It is an alternative, not to quietude, but to violent protest.

- Peaceful protest cannot be stopped, or may be stopped only by disproportionate means or effort.

5. *Under what conditions do you believe that the state could be justified in censuring or prohibiting the free expression and exchange of information and opinion?*

What does ECHR tell us here? Firstly, it puts opinion and information together under the heading of 'freedom of expression'. Secondly, it declares this to be a qualified right, and gives a large number of headings under which it might be violated. Headings, however, are not reasons, and phrases like 'national security' or 'the protection of health and morals' are very general.

Some libertarian-minded folk might believe that state censorship or prohibition of any kind can never be justified, except possibly under wartime conditions when national survival is at stake. We do not find this is a complete answer. Firstly, ECHR disagrees with it. Secondly, we have an inkling that inside even the most apparently liberal-minded and tolerant person is a censor waiting to emerge, if only the right button can be pressed. Let us see if we can press it. Here are two examples to mull over, to which we will return in our chapter on freedom of expression.

Racial abuse. Strong-minded libertarians might claim that freedom of expression should be absolute, at least in so far as it does not lead by means of a direct and inexorable causal chain to damage to others. John Stuart Mill might have argued for freedom of expression in this area, along the following lines:

- racial abuse is based upon racial prejudice;

- racial prejudice is inherently irrational;

- irrational opinion should be exposed to the light of day, in order that it may be countered and corrected by a more rational view;

- therefore, racially prejudiced people should be free (within some constraints, perhaps those of the common law) to express their views.

Clearly, there is a contrary view. There are major issues here about the nature of a multi-racial and multi-cultural society, of which Mill was not a member. We have raised the issue to show that there is a possible argument, and to indicate at least one area in which the possibility of censorship or prohibition of freedom of expression may be countenanced by people who might otherwise be generally opposed to it.

Censorship of paedophilia. Even in a broad-minded, inclusive and tolerant society there are some interests that are beyond the pale. There would appear to be a consensus of opinion (except, of course, amongst paedophiles) that paedophilia is one of them. We suppose that there is a very strong body of opinion that paedophilia should be opposed by a variety of means, including censorship. That censorship should include the prohibition of the freedoms of expression and association of paedophiles on the Internet, despite the major practical difficulties that this aim imposes in an age of instant and mass communication.

This topic raises some very tricky issues in regard to the necessity and proportionality of the measures taken in order to achieve a legitimate aim. These are concepts that we have not yet begun to explore in any depth, but with which, by the end of the book, you will be deeply familiar!

2

Human rights in the UK

The UK has until recently held an ambivalent attitude to human rights. We may account for this ambivalence in terms of three inter-related factors: national character, the development of our system of law, and our national history.

COMMON LAW

The British (as opposed, for example, to the French) are popularly supposed to be sceptical of grand philosophical schemes and solutions and essentially pragmatic in their approach to solving problems. Thus France has the Code Napoleon, which lists all criminal offences and prescribes the penalties that attach to them. And what is our equivalent to this high-level doctrine? The common law, which is no equivalent at all, but the phrase used to describe the unwritten traditions of the people as recorded and interpreted by their professional judges.

Some of those judges may on occasion achieve a certain eloquence, even a level of quasi-mystical rhetoric which negates its own denial – 'It is a custom recognized from time immemorial', for example, said the wonderful Lord Justice Denning, 'that private schools may demand their fees termly and in advance' – but the product is not a Code Napoleon. Neither common law nor statute law – law created by parliament – sets out to cover every eventuality on a pre-planned basis. The law has developed as people have needed it, and it is clustered where it is most needed. The criminal law has developed around the most frequently committed crimes, and those that do the most harm. We must also suppose, in order for us to lower the tone of this so far edifying paragraph before you do so in our place, that it is also clustered around those crimes that produce the greatest earnings for lawyers: but we hope that there is some correlation between these three factors. The criminal law is a largely pragmatic solution to the largely practical problems of crime and disorder. Civil law has likewise developed to deal with commonly intransigent problems in regard to property, contracts, wills and so on.

We must also acknowledge, before some perspicacious reader does so for us, that the English have from time to time made some sort of declaration of rights as the spirit moved them. Thus we have the Magna Carta of 1415 and the Bill of Rights of 1689. Are these not in themselves proof that the English are in fact rights-conscious? They show that some rights have on occasion been declared: but we would argue that this has occurred only in periods of crisis, and the declarations in question have been more in the nature of a symbolic gesture than the creation of a comprehensive framework of rights. Once the crisis was past, the English have thankfully reverted to their traditional prag-matism, and there has been no creation of a written constitution and comprehensive bill of rights.

The common law and human rights

Where, then, do rights fit into our legal system and traditions? Rights are discernible in the law, but they are usually implicit rather than explicit. A robust defender of the common law might argue that the whole concept of 'rights' is unnecessary, and could prove counter-productive. The common law jurist does not need a right to life to be declared, for example, in order for him to know that killing people is wrong. The Bible tells him that it is wrong. Perhaps even more importantly, so do his community, his family, his conscience and his experience – and the common law has developed accordingly.

The result of the considerable attention having been given to homicide over a considerable time is that we have a very extensive body of legal wisdom in this area. For example, we can distinguish between murder and manslaughter, and award different penalties accordingly.

Because they used to be commonplace offences, we recognize infanticide and child destruction as distinct crimes, worthy of distinct attention. We may achieve a high degree of sophistication in considering the mental state and degree of responsibility of the accused person, as our knowledge of psychology has developed over time and this has affected the law, and so on. In other words, we have gone beyond the basic confines of a right to life, and the common law at its best allows for a richer and more flexible interpretation of people's needs than any bare scrap of doctrine.

The right to a fair trial

The right to a fair trial is a fundamental principle of British justice. Our understanding of what is meant by a fair trial was not laid down by a Napoleon, but has evolved over the centuries and is still evolving now. It has the consent of the public as a living agreement that has been tried and tested in response to contemporary needs and pressures, and it may change in the future. We know the features of a fair trial, then, because – if you will forgive the pun – they have emerged from trial and error; and that is the pragmatic argument in a nutshell. Other nations protect the rights of the citizen in theory, by means of declarations and constitutions: common law jurisdictions protect them in practice, by everyday decisions in the courts which rest upon the integrity, wisdom and discretion of the judges, as well as by our other mechanisms for protecting freedoms.

The traditional view on human rights, therefore, if we may exaggerate things a little for the sake of exposition, is that they are foreign, over-schematic and in any case unnecessary. The Briton has no need of them, and an insistence upon them may in fact prove to his disadvantage, for under a system in which certain rights are declared and protected by law, no other rights may be claimed to exist. The ordinary citizen's rights are protected by the common law, by parliament, and by the British constitution as a whole – that wonderful if unwritten set of agreements and understandings, all the more powerful for being carried in the hearts and minds of its subjects rather than remaining the esoteric resource of constitutional lawyers, which no government dare transgress, and which protects our real rights far more effectively than any mere code.

This view cannot be dissociated from Britain's national history, with its long tradition of peace, stability, economic progress and freedom from invasion. England's last military government was under Oliver Cromwell, who died in 1658; and despite both his military successes and his firm stand on what had not yet become known as 'sleaze' – he was against it – the military government was a thoroughly unpopular one. Britons retain a strong belief in the importance of the freedom of the citizen against the arbitrary power of the state, which has been recognized from time to time in some of the more memorable utterances of our judges, in parliamentary speeches, in the press, in our literature, and perhaps most importantly in our actions. We do not need rights.

This view was still very much in evidence in 1948, when the UN produced its UDHR, to be followed up immediately by the Council of Europe's ECHR, which gave a remedy against the abuse of specified rights, and promoted fundamental freedoms.

British lawyers were instrumental in the drafting of that convention, and indeed it was intended to represent the best understanding of human rights and fundamental freedoms that had emerged under the common law to that point. ECHR was the essence of common law, and a Europe that had been savaged by dictatorship and totalitarianism was much in need of it. The UK, however, was not. Briton's rights were protected under the common law, into which the ECHR was not incorporated. Indeed, British subjects would not have the right to plead a breach of their human rights, even at Strasbourg, until 1966, when Harold Wilson's government allowed the right of individual petition to the European Court – a development presumably not unconnected with the demise of the British empire, and the decreasing likelihood that its subjects would take their grievances over imperial legislation and its effects on their national and personal freedom to the ECtHR.

THE CURRENT VIEW

The traditional view that the UK did not and does not need to incorporate ECHR into domestic law is, of course, wrong. Or rather, to use the more careful words of the government's White Paper on the subject, which preceded the Human Rights Act (HRA) of 1998: it has not stood the test of time. *Rights Brought Home* (The Home Office, 1997) is an excellent read, and we will quote from it. But it does not give the whole picture. Why, 50 years after it had helped to create the ECHR, did the British government finally decide to bring those rights home? We know why it did not do so in 1950. We do not yet know why it did do so in 2000 – when the HRA came into effect in the UK as a whole.

Rights Brought Home

The official answer is to be found in *Rights Brought Home,* which carefully blended pragmatism and ideals. It stated that human rights were important and should be effectively upheld, for which the current mechanisms were inadequate. Taking a case to Strasbourg took too long and was too expensive. Those rights should be argued for in a domestic court. This would allow

British judges to comment upon human rights issues and contribute to human rights law in this important area, rather than remaining outsiders to a major body of European law. To bring rights home would correct any false impression in mainland Europe of a lack of respect for human rights within British jurisdiction.

Are these the complete reasons why the UK now has the HRA? Probably not. It is hard to believe that politicians, unlike the people who vote for them, are always and only inspired by the purest of motives, and there may have been an element of enlightened self-interest in (New) Labour's conversion to human rights. Between 1979 and 1997 Labour had lost four elections in a row, and were beginning to wonder if they were unelectable. They perceived the need to go into partnership with the Liberal Democrats in order to win power. The Liberal Democrats were heavily committed to human rights. On that basis, Labour's conversion to the need for the incorporation of human rights into domestic law makes sense as a political bargaining counter as well as a move to be argued for on its own merits. Offer human rights, and you win the liberals' cooperation. Oppose or ignore it, and you don't. (We are indebted to Professor Laurence Lustgarten of the University of Southampton's law faculty for this historical insight.)

Political calculation may be taken into account, but it is not the whole answer. Labour officially adopted human rights in 1993 when it was led by John Smith, who saw a need to offer the citizen or subject a greater protection against the powers of the state, and a human rights act as the easiest available means to achieve this end. It was a less radical measure than to declare a bill of rights, for which some had lobbied, but there was still an element of idealism in its adoption.

In the end the HRA was passed because it had become part of the agenda of the Labour Party, partly for ideological and partly for pragmatic reasons, and perhaps partly because it represented the spirit of the times. The UK was isolated in not having incorporated the ECHR into domestic law. Its government was embarrassed at having its domestic issues discussed at Strasbourg, thereby creating a false impression of the UK's attitude to human rights, when they might have been resolved with far less fuss and bother at home. Moreover, New Labour had declared itself to be committed to an ethical foreign policy and had acted overseas, at least in some cases, in order to protect human rights. How odd that Britons should be prepared to fight for something overseas that they had not apparently guaranteed at home! The lobbying of groups such as the British Institute for Human Rights had some effect; and the judiciary itself, traditionally that most conservative of institutions and the bastion of the common law, had come to represent a much broader range of opinion.

The HRA: a compromise between extremes

At the end of the day, we may see the Act as a compromise. On the one hand, it allows us to plead our rights in domestic courts, which was not possible before. It creates the possibility for the constitutional criticism of Acts of parliament by the judiciary in that they are perceived to be incompatible with human rights. And it has been declared by the government itself to be the beginning of a process of creating a human rights culture in the UK – a culture that the government wishes to see develop. To that extent it could be described as a revolutionary act, if a very quiet one.

On the other hand, we could argue that the rights protected are limited in range to the prevention of wholesale violations of basic liberties. There is little or no mention of social and economic rights in the ECHR, including its various protocols – not all of which have in any case been signed by the British government and ratified at Westminster. Moreover, the nature and extent of even those rights that are guaranteed have been subjected to a fairly cautious and respectful interpretation by the European Commission and the ECtHR during their lengthy existence.

Finally, it could be argued that it is convenient, to say the least, that Europe has created the doctrine of a 'margin of interpretation' by means of which Strasbourg is sometimes able to recognize and declare that a variation in attitude towards the nature and extent of a right, between one European country and another, is not necessarily a breach of human rights, but may be allowed for under national variation.

Judges are unlikely to be either reckless or rash in the exercise of their wider powers as protectors of the citizen or subject against the state, since they will not wish to enter the political arena without very good cause. We doubt that they will be very fast off the mark in their declarations of incompatibility.

As to the government itself: it is easily possible to interpret its actions in terms of a compromise. We may consider the utterances of various ministers themselves, including those responsible for both law and order, who on occasion appear to be in need of a gentle reminder that the HRA has been passed! In addition, we may review the government's structural activities. The government has so far failed to set up a Human Rights Commission for the UK, or to appoint a Commissioner. (There is a Human Rights Commissioner in Northern Ireland, but that creation was independent of the HRA.) Indeed, Westminster still lacks a Human Rights Select Committee. In reality, human rights are protected by the usual jumble sale of bargains, compromises and understandings by which a pragmatic organization seeks to remedy obvious abuses while at the same time avoiding radical reform.

A pragmatic way forward

In our view the government has chosen to bring human rights into the system in a way that tries to avoid the traps encountered elsewhere, and without being too doctrinaire about the whole process. It has benefited by considering the experience of states such as Canada and New Zealand, both of which have brought in human rights in different ways; and it has sought out a realistic way to achieve its main objective. We believe that the consequences of this Act will be profound, and that at least some of them will not have been catered for in the preliminary planning. But we are inclined to agree that this will be a quiet revolution. Before we go on to develop that theme any further, however, it is time that we offered a brief word on how the new Act is intended to operate; and this will be the subject of the next chapter.

QUESTIONS

Please choose the answer that you think closest to the truth.

1. Why was the Council of Europe set up?

    (a) To promote European economic union.

    (b) To establish a common system of justice throughout Europe.

    (c) To promote the ideals of a democratic society within Europe.

    (d) To establish a European defence force.

2. What are the three pillars of the Council of Europe?

    (a) Human rights, pluralist democracy, and trial by jury.

    (b) Human rights, parliamentary sovereignty, and trial by jury.

    (c) Human rights, the rule of law, and parliamentary sovereignty.

    (d) Human rights, the rule of law, and pluralist democracy.

True or false?

3. The European Convention on Human Rights (ECHR) forbids slavery.

4. ECHR forbids torture.

5. ECHR forbids false imprisonment.

6. ECHR guarantees the right to work.

7. ECHR guarantees the right to a fair wage.

8. ECHR guarantees freedom from discrimination.

9. ECHR guarantees the freedom of the press.

10. ECHR guarantees the right to marry.

ANSWERS

1. *Why was the Council of Europe set up?*
   The answer is (c).

2. *What are the three pillars of the Council of Europe?*
   The answer is (d).

3. *The European Convention on Human Rights (ECHR) forbids slavery.*
   True. Slavery is absolutely prohibited.

4. *ECHR forbids torture.*
   True. Torture is absolutely prohibited.

5. *ECHR forbids false imprisonment.*
   False. ECHR guarantees both the right to a fair trial and the right not be subjected to *ex post facto* legislation. We may, perhaps, assume that the proper observation of these rights will prevent false imprisonment, but that right is not guaranteed. However, if there is a common law tradition that we should not be falsely imprisoned, then the HRA does not remove that right by not mentioning it. All previous rights remain in existence.

6. _ECHR guarantees the right to work._
   False. ECHR contains no social and economic rights.

7. _ECHR guarantees the right to a fair wage._
   False. ECHR contains no social and economic rights.

8. _ECHR guarantees freedom from discrimination._
   True – although only in regard to the other rights it guarantees.

9. _ECHR guarantees the freedom of the press._
   False. ECHR guarantees freedom of expression as a qualified right. We think it would be stretching the text too far to say that this means that ECHR guarantees the freedom of the press.

10. _ECHR guarantees the right to marry._
    True.

Commentary

We hope that you enjoyed and benefited from this exercise, and that it will have begun to help you to think like a lawyer. Close analysis of ECHR is beneficial, as it enables us to begin to perceive the formal limitations and conceptual possibilities of the rights and freedoms it guarantees. It is important to recognize that most rights are qualified.

3

A short guide to the Human Rights Act, 1998

We need to understand the Human Rights Act (HRA) itself. We need to know how it is constructed, and how it is intended to work: what it will achieve, and what it will not achieve. On the face of it, that task is a relatively simple one, but we think it will be sufficiently challenging! The Act is quite short, is relatively easy to read, and is divided into 19 sections, not all of which need concern us here. We shall include in our analysis the White Paper, *Rights Brought Home* (The Home Office, 1997) to which we have already referred in the previous chapter, since without its comments the Act itself does not always make sense. We will divide this chapter into three areas: exploration, comment and application. Please bear in mind that our exploration will not go into the depth necessary in a legal textbook, as it would defeat our purpose here of making the Act accessible.

A DUTY TO UPHOLD HUMAN RIGHTS (HRA, SECTION 6)

All public authorities must respect and uphold human rights in the course of their actions. This is a double obligation, both negative and positive. Negatively, the public authority must not violate human rights. Positively, it must uphold them. (Section 6 actually states that it is unlawful for a public authority to act in such a way that is incompatible with a Convention right. In strengthening this definition, we have taken into account both *Rights Brought Home* and the lessons of Strasbourg case law in this area.)

What is a public authority?

Perhaps oddly, the HRA does not tell us the answer to this. The White Paper gives us some examples of organizations that are public authorities, such as the courts and the police, and some examples of organizations that are not. It then introduces the notion of a hybrid authority, which is not so easily classified. Hybrid authorities carry out some business for themselves and some on behalf of the state. An example would be Group 4, the private security company. When this organization is conveying privately owned bullion to a privately owned vault, it is working as a private company. When, on the other hand, it is conveying prisoners to a court, it is operating in a public capacity and is directly answerable for its behaviour in terms of human rights. Other examples of hybrid authorities would include the Financial Services Authority, the Legal Aid Board, the BBC, Railtrack and NHS trusts.

Some organizations are inherently difficult to classify, and some have caused confusion even to ministers – as is revealed in the parliamentary debates on the passage of the HRA, when the question of the status of the Press Complaints Commission arose. The press itself is a private institution, in that although in some of its activities it operates or claims to operate in the public interest, the government or state does not own it. However, it is arguable that the Press Complaints Commission is a public authority, at least in hybrid terms.

Why has the government made this awkward and potentially confusing distinction, when it might have said that the HRA applied generally? For a mixture of reasons, which we suspect will become apparent as the chapter progresses, and to which we shall return in our evaluation.

Testing for public authority status

What test might a court adopt in order to determine whether or not a particular organization is, or is acting as, a public authority? There are a number of possibilities:

▮ A public authority may be seen as 'an emanation of the state'. (This is the test of the European Court of Justice, which deals with EC matters.) Such an institution – for example, we would suppose, an unemployment benefit office – provides a service in order to carry out a function of the state. It has special powers to carry out such a service, and it is under the control of the state. It is therefore a public authority.

▮ The Datafin definition may be applied (*R v. Panel on Takeovers and Mergers, ex parte Datafin plc* [1987] 1 QB 814 (CA)).

▮ A body is likely to be classified as a public authority if:

  – the government would intervene in its absence;

  – the government supports its work in some way, for example by weaving it into legislation or by giving it certain powers (consider RSPCA or NSPCC);

  – the body exercises monopolistic powers in the public sphere (for example, the British Boxing Board of Control, or other national sporting bodies); or

– the aggrieved person agrees to submit to the jurisdiction of such a body (for example, licensing authorities).

▌ A new test may be devised and applied.

Parliament itself is exempted from the HRA. Why? Because it wishes to preserve its sovereignty, and that is such an important concept that it deserves its own section.

Parliamentary sovereignty

Parliamentary sovereignty, the separation of powers and the importance of trial by jury, are some of the most important foundation stones of our constitution. In theory, parliament is supreme, and may make any law that it chooses. No one and nothing is above parliament, and it is answerable to no one save the electorate at a general election. We say 'in theory' because of our membership of the European Community, but let us put that to one side for the moment. Parliament recognizes no superior authority outside Brussels, at any rate, and this means that the judiciary cannot be allowed to balk its will.

Human rights might conflict with this. Say, for example, that parliament wished to raise a tax that deducted part of our hard-gained earnings from us, either at source or through the compulsory payment of a tax on our income on some regular basis. (We know that this is a fanciful idea, but please bear with us.) We should, of course, object immediately to such an outrageous imposition, and send it back whence it came forthwith; but let us suppose that we as citizens and electors have tolerated it.

Along comes human rights, and a judge declares that the taxation of income is unconstitutional because it violates the ordinary citizen's right to the peaceful enjoyment of his possessions. Not so, says the government: it needs the revenue obtained from income tax to achieve the general good.

The collective good is of no interest to my client, says the lawyer: she is only concerned with her individual gain and loss, and it is far from clear that the general good, even if it is being achieved, is to her particular advantage.

Parliament, replies parliament, is sovereign because it represents the will of the people. It is not the place of unelected judges to question the will of the people as expressed through their elected representatives, and which is intended to achieve social justice.

And there the debate pauses, for the judges will accept this argument and in the absence of a written constitution, bill of rights, or supreme court, parliament is indeed sovereign. To what extent will the HRA affect this? That is a question to which we return later. But first we need to look at the mechanics of the Act by examining some of its sections.

SECTION 1

Section 1 states which parts of ECHR have been incorporated into the new Act. It includes Articles 2 to 12 and Article 14 of ECHR. In addition, the Act includes Articles 1 to 3 of the First Protocol and Articles 1 and 2 of the Sixth Protocol as read with Articles 16 to 18 of the Convention. For reference, the full text is to be found in Chapter 11 of this book.

A note on protocols

A protocol is an addition to an Act. In order for it to have the same status of the Act, ie to be legally binding, it needs to be both signed and ratified by the states that had agreed to the Act itself. A government may sign a protocol with a view to later ratification by its representative assembly. Until that protocol is ratified it is a declaration of intent and is not legally binding. There are a number of protocols to ECHR, and the UK has accepted some and left others alone.

The missing articles

Article 1 of ECHR has not been incorporated. This article states that the High Contracting Parties shall secure to everyone within their jurisdiction the rights and freedoms defined thereafter. It was stated in parliamentary debate that the HRA is itself a guarantee for Article 1.

Article 13 is also excluded, for the same reason. This is paraphrased as the right to an effective remedy, and states that:

> *everyone whose rights and freedoms as set forth in this Convention are violated shall have an effective remedy before a national authority notwithstanding that the violation has been committed by persons acting in an official capacity.*

Both articles will still affect British jurisprudence. First, Section 2 (HRA) states that Strasbourg case law should be taken into account in human rights deliberations in British courts, and that case law includes cases that refer to articles 1 and 13. Secondly, the appellant can still take his case to Strasbourg once he has exhausted domestic remedies, and there raise issues in regard to any article included in ECHR, whether or not it has been included in HRA.

SECTION 2

Section 2 states that a court or tribunal determining a question that has arisen in connection with a Convention right must take into account any relevant ECHR decisions.

Comment

The phrase 'take into account' is carefully chosen. *Rights Brought Home* states specifically that ECHR decisions will not be binding on domestic courts. However, we may expect them to be persuasive.

SECTION 3

So far as it is possible to do so, primary and subordinate legislation must be read and given effect in a way that is compatible with the convention rights.

SECTION 4

If a specified court finds that its work is impossible because it cannot read specific legislation to be compatible with human rights, then it may make a declaration of incompatibility in regard to that legislation. Even if it makes such a declaration, however, the law still holds until parliament chooses to change it; and the court must continue to apply the law.

SECTION 5

It is unlawful for a public authority to act in such a way that is incompatible with a Convention right. However, such a restriction does not apply if the public authority was compelled to do so by primary legislation or its effects.

INTERPRETING LEGISLATION PURPOSIVELY

Under Section 3 of the HRA, any court must strive to interpret existing legislation in such a way that it is compatible with human rights. In order to do this, the court may need to interpret a statute purposively, or even, to use one of philosophy's favourite words, teleologically. What on earth does this mean? Actually, the idea is quite simple, although its exercise may lead to argument. It means that the court that is interpreting the law should bear in mind what the law is trying to achieve, rather than simply to confine its thoughts to a literal interpretation of its words.

The Bail Act

For example, let us consider the Bail Act, which requires or appears to require a magistrate to refuse bail under certain conditions. The magistrate's literal reading of those conditions could lead to a situation in which the rights of the accused person to liberty and security under Article 5 of the ECHR are at least threatened, if not breached outright. However, if the magistrate reads the Bail Act purposively, and thereby exercises a human rights-conscious discretion as to whether or not he awards bail, he may avoid that situation, and ensure that his acts are both lawful and congruent with human rights.

What is the significance of purposive interpretation, as far as our discussion of the constitutional significance of the HRA is concerned? What does it have to do with the role of the judges? Quite simply, we believe that this section of the Act is designed to eliminate or at least reduce radical constitutional conflict. It allows the judiciary, from the working level of the magistracy to the upper echelons of the higher courts, to carry out their task of interpreting and applying the law with respect both for what parliament intended and for human rights.

How will it work in practice? We are sorry to use this phrase so early in the book, but for the moment, we will have to wait and see.

Judicial review

A decision by a public authority may be the object of judicial review. Traditionally, judges have confined that review to examining the lawfulness and overall rationality of the decision. In regard to rationality, the only decisions they were prepared to challenge were those deemed to be manifestly irrational – which was naturally a small number.

A decision by a public authority should be the applied wisdom of experts in the area, wherever it might be, that required a decision. Judges were experts in the law. They were not experts in planning, medical administration, or any other subject outside the law's boundaries, and nor were they in possession of the relevant information; and it was not appropriate that they should review what might be called the internal logic of such decisions. What is the distinction here? It can be made clearer by means of a hypothetical example.

Opening the sports centre

Suppose that a local authority decides not to open a municipal sports centre on a Sunday, because it recognizes that those local people who are strict religious observers would be offended were the centre to be opened. The decision is reviewed and left to stand because it is not manifestly irrational. The recognition of religious beliefs and principles is a valid basis for making a decision, and it would not necessarily be invalidated were it to be shown, for example, that in another part of the country a municipally-owned sports centre *were* open on a Sunday. Local government rests upon the principle that it is local, and what the electors may accept in one part of the country may be very different from what is acceptable in another area.

We are left to ponder the question: what would be an unacceptable decision? The test of manifest irrationality is a very weak one and does not seem to rule out very much, apart from pure capriciousness or obvious malice or prejudice. But before we spend too much time in wrestling with that conundrum, let us move on, as the whole argument itself has done under the impact of human rights legislation.

We may summarize informed speculation about the impact of the HRA on judicial review as follows. The old argument would be that the role of the judges in this area is clear. They are experts only in law, and not in decision-making and administration. Moreover, they are not elected and are not amenable to public opinion. It is right and proper that they should be used to prevent or correct manifest irrationality and no more.

The new argument is that the HRA changes this familiar and settled interpretation of the proper role of the judiciary. Judges must now protect human rights in everything that they do, and that includes judicial review. In addition to the general principles that they apply in reviewing a decision, which centre on its general rationality, they must look to see that it protects and upholds human rights and does not work against them.

Let us return to our example of the sports centre and review it in terms of human rights doctrine. On the one hand, the members of Group A have a right to respect for their religious views. If they are offended that municipal facilities towards which they contribute as ratepayers are used on a Sunday, then that sense of offence should be taken into account.

On the other hand we have another group of people who may not share the same religious conviction as the first group, or who have a different slant upon Christianity. Group B would like to exercise their right to freedom of expression and assembly on a Sunday, and might also claim that the prohibition of that exercise violates other rights as well.

Which group is right? Possibly neither, in absolute terms. The rights being discussed here are qualified, and there is a balancing of interests to be carried out. However, the bedrock notion of proportionality would appear highly applicable in this case. Is it really necessary to close the sports centre on a Sunday in order to respect the religious susceptibilities of Group A? They are not being forced to desecrate the Sabbath, which they may continue to recognize in whatever way they choose: but their right to choose and to practise their religion does not give them the right to impose it on others, and thereby violate others' rights.

Is there not a practical solution that could be found in this situation, which would allow for the peaceful expression of differentiated interests? We suspect that there is: and if the local government in question is unable or unwilling to make the effort to find it, then it is appropriate that the disproportionate policy on which they have decided in its absence should be reviewed by other parties, even if unelected.

Here, however, we are leaping ahead of reality in our enthusiasm. We opine that the HRA will in the long run make judicial review a rather more rigorous process than it has been in the past and that the consequences of this for managerial decision-making will need to be taken into account.

The margin of appreciation

This is an ECHR doctrine that could be misapplied in domestic courts, and it needs to be understood in its Strasbourg context.

The ECtHR was _not_ set up to create a uniform system of justice throughout Europe. If we take, for example, two geographically close neighbours, the UK and France, they would appear to operate very different systems of justice. Thus, one system is broadly adversarial and the other inquisitorial. One system regards the jury as the best safeguard for the rights of the common man and the other does not. One system uses lay magistrates and promotes its judges from the ranks of successful barristers, whereas the other has a professional corps of specialist judges; and so on. (We might, of course, have added that one system conducts its proceedings in English and the other in French; a difference so taken for granted that we had ignored it – and yet, what could be more different?)

However, as far as Strasbourg is concerned, whatever the real or apparent differences between these two systems, they are both capable of respecting human rights and both capable of achieving justice. The articles of the ECHR float as higher order principles over the actual proceedings in any court. Whatever the crime of which the defendant is accused, and whatever the process followed to investigate the accusation, he has a right to a fair trial; and that trial must respect certain principles that may be discerned in the judicial process of any member state of the Council of Europe.

Inessential differences between systems may be noted but left alone by Strasbourg as falling within the confines of the 'margin of appreciation', a phrase whose origins were French and which would, perhaps, have been better translated as the 'margin of discretion'.

The different mores of European societies may also be taken into account in Strasbourg. Indeed, it would be impossible for the ECHR to operate without some recognition of national difference. What may be accepted in Sweden in regard to the open display of homosexual affection, for example, might be far from acceptable in Malta or Turkey; and yet all three countries are equal members of the Council of Europe. Where there is no general agreement across Europe as to what constitutes acceptable behaviour, or where the values of one part of Europe differ markedly from another, then the ECtHR will not set a standard unless it finds that fundamental human rights are irretrievably breached. Where it is possible to tolerate national differences, it will do so; and it may be, although this is hypothesis on our part, that the Strasbourg judges expect the mature, long-industrialized, liberal-minded democracies of Western Europe to show a greater social tolerance than other societies.

The point of our exploration so far, however, is not to go into great depth on national differences, interesting as that might be. What we must emphasize is that the margin of appreciation is, in our view, a doctrine that can only be used in Strasbourg. It is *not* available for use within a state.

Let us suppose that a magistrate in Gloucestershire, for example, issues an injunction banning a supposedly pornographic exhibition. That exhibition has already been shown in London without any great offence being taken. The magistrate cannot claim an internal margin of appreciation within England on the basis that attitudes in the cosmopolis are always more advanced than those in the country. Rights are rights, and the Justice of the Peace should respect them. A Gloucestershire ban may only be justified if the exhibition is likely to lead to a breach of the peace, and even then an outright ban may not be proportionate.

In essence, then, the margin of appreciation is the discretion afforded to ECtHR judges in reviewing decisions made under different judicial systems. It is not available for internal use.

QUESTIONS

True or false?

1. HRA incorporates the whole of ECHR into domestic law.

2. The incorporation of ECHR into domestic law will mean the end of common law.

3. HRA empowers any court to challenge any Act of parliament as being incompatible with human rights. Once such a challenge has been made that Act may no longer be enforced as law.

4. If an Act of parliament is declared to be incompatible with human rights, it must be amended by parliament forthwith.

5. Under HRA, all decisions made by the ECtHR at Strasbourg are binding on British courts.

6. HRA does not protect people living in the UK or any of its dependent territories who are not British citizens.

Case studies

7. *Authority.* The HRA states that all public authorities must act in accordance with the Act.

   – What is a public authority?

   – What is a hybrid authority?

   – How would you classify the organization for which you work? In broad terms, is it public or private?

   – If it is not a public authority, under what circumstances would you accept the classification that it is acting as a hybrid authority?

   – To what extent is the organization prepared for this classification and its consequences in terms of its responsibilities both as an employer and supplier of goods and services?

8. *Rights at work.* You believe that your rights have been violated at work, and you wish to raise a grievance about this. However, your employer tells you that his is a private business, and it is thus not bound by the HRA. *What do you do next?*

ANSWERS

1. *HRA incorporates the whole of ECHR into domestic law.*
   False. Part of ECHR is given further effect by HRA.

2. *The incorporation of ECHR into domestic law will mean the end of common law.*
   False. Both government and legal profession agree that the common law will grow and develop as a result of HRA.

3. *HRA empowers any court to challenge any Act of parliament as being incompatible with human rights. Once such a challenge has been made, that Act may no longer be enforced as law.*
   False. Only specified higher courts may declare an Act of parliament to be incompatible with HRA. Even if such a declaration is made that law must continue to be enforced.

4. *If an Act of parliament is declared to be incompatible with human rights, it must be amended by parliament forthwith.*
   False. Under the doctrine of parliamentary sovereignty, parliament retains a choice.

5. *Under HRA, all decisions made by the ECtHR at Strasbourg are binding on British courts.*
   False. They are not binding. They must be taken into account.

6. *HRA does not protect people living in the UK or any of its dependent territories who are not British citizens.*
   False. HRA covers anyone, citizen, subject or refugee, residing under British jurisdiction. However, we must note two points: the rights of aliens are restricted by ECHR, and the rights of immigrants and refugees have been very carefully interpreted, for example in regard to family life.

7. *Authority.*
   These questions are best answered by means of careful appraisal by the reader and do not lend themselves to an authoritative solution.

8. *Rights at work.*

Again, we cannot give a definitive answer. However, we can make some suggestions. You have a range of options open to you, both legal and non-legal. You might:

– Challenge the statement that HRA does not apply, by claiming that your company carries out certain of its duties on behalf of the state and therefore is subject to HRA.

– Manage to bring your case before a court or tribunal. This must take HRA into account, even if the reason why the case came to court in the first place was not ostensibly to do with human rights.

– Consider the code of ethics of your company and claim that the management should be guided by it in this case and therefore address your grievance.

– Publicize the issue concerned as of general human rights interest, and seek redress of grievance by this means.

4

How to interpret and apply human rights

Within ECHR, there are two main types of rights: absolute and qualified. It is essential to know the difference and how the two operate.

ABSOLUTE HUMAN RIGHTS

Absolute rights are easily described, comparatively simple to interpret, and few in number. Here is the clearest example:

No one shall be subjected to torture or to inhuman or degrading treatment or punishment. (ECHR, Article 3)

This is the shortest article in ECHR. It is wholly unqualified. Both torture and inhuman or degrading treatment or punishment is absolutely prohibited, with no ifs, buts or maybes. There are no conditions under which the deliberate infliction of torture or inhuman or degrading treatment may be justified, even in order to save the lives of others. What might otherwise be discussed as fascinating moral dilemmas have no place in human rights discourse. We cannot, for example, argue that it is justified to inflict severe pain on A in order to save B, or even in order to save 100 Bs. This applies even under the most extreme of circumstances, such as when A, a lifelong criminal, is taunting the state with its inability to prevent a further murder on his part.

The reasons for this absolute prohibition are very clear. Firstly, ECHR was drafted after World War II in order to prevent a repetition of the excesses of organizations such as the Gestapo, to whom torture was a commonplace. Secondly, since human rights cannot be given away, even the person who grossly attacks the rights of others, such as the kidnapper, retains his own rights. Thirdly, the recognition that the infliction of torture or inhuman and degrading treatment may be justified under the most extreme and unusual circumstances, is the beginning of a slippery slope towards its general recognition.

The issue then becomes one of deciding what reaches the threshold of torture or inhuman or degrading treatment. ECHR has set the threshold high so that this prohibition retains its integrity, and the Commission has rejected any frivolous claims of torture or inhuman and degrading treatment, although it is always concerned to discover the precise circumstances that apply when this offence is alleged. (Thus, a particularly vulnerable person might find something to be inhuman and degrading, which another recipient would not.)

In essence, the term 'torture' means any act by which severe pain and suffering, whether physical or mental, is intentionally inflicted on a person for such purposes as obtaining from him or a third person information or confession, punishing him for an act he or a third person has committed or is suspected of having committed, or intimidating or coercing him or a third person. It does not include pain or suffering arising only from, inherent in or incidental to lawful sanctions. The imposition of the death penalty in time or threat of war, which is allowed under the Convention, does not violate Article 3. Nor does the pain or suffering arising from a medical operation count as torture – unless it were the doctor's intention simply to inflict severe pain, rather than to carry out an operation for normal medical purposes.

Other absolute or unqualified articles are Article 4.1, which states that no one shall be held in slavery or servitude, and Article 9.1, which states that everyone has the right to freedom of thought, conscience and religion. All other rights or parts of rights (including 4.2 and 9.2) are either qualified or limited. Article 7 is sometimes described as absolute, and certainly the freedom from punishment without law is a most important one. However, there is a qualifying paragraph – what might be called the 'Nuremberg exception'. There is no absolute justification in simply obeying orders, or respecting an oath – as some war criminals claimed to be doing at Nuremberg. In this area ECHR needs to be read with other international treaties and agreements which go on to specify in greater detail what is and is not acceptable behaviour for state officials.

QUALIFIED RIGHTS

The classic qualified rights are Articles 8, 9 (seen as a whole), 10 and 11, all of which take the same form. First of all, a right is asserted. Then are described the circumstances under which a public authority might seek to justify its violation of the right in question. It is important to note that:

▧ Both the rights themselves, and the circumstances under which they may be violated, are expressed in general terms.

▧ The qualifying circumstances which accompany the four articles are similar, but not the same. Some offer more possibilities than others.

▧ It is necessary to look to case law to see how those circumstances have been interpreted and applied in court.

▧ It is wise at the same time to remember that ECHR is a living instrument and that Strasbourg is not bound by its previous decisions. For example, the definition of the threshold of inhuman and degrading treatment may change over time. We must also emphasize that under the HRA, ECHR decisions must be taken into account in British courts. However, they are not binding. (Decisions from other jurisdictions such as South Africa or New Zealand in which relevant human rights issues have been raised and addressed within a similar common law system, may also be quoted.)

ECtHR does not set out to provide specific guidance to public authorities as to how the articles should be interpreted and applied. Still less does it set out to recommend a pan-European legal system. Strasbourg is an international tribunal and does not exist to produce a common European system of justice. It is concerned to ensure that the same principles are applied in all systems.

What are those principles, as they have emerged in case law? They may be inferred as follows:

▮ legality;

▮ accountability;

▮ necessity;

▮ proportionality.

Legality

Limitations on this freedom must be 'prescribed by law' – Article 9.

The actions of the public authority must be based on written and accessible law, regulations or procedures. Impromptu actions may be arbitrary, unfair or biased. They may be unpredictable. They do not, in any case, allow the citizen to know what the state is and is not entitled to do.

In the context of the right to a fair criminal trial, legality includes the notion of being able to foresee the consequences of one's actions. Everyone has the right to know what is and is not lawful, so that he may regulate his conduct accordingly. If he were charged with an offence that he did not and could not know to be unlawful, then his human rights would be violated.

In addition, the activities of the state must be regulated in regard to the measures that it takes in order to combat unlawful activity, if those measures in themselves could constitute a breach of human rights. Someone who is contemplating a criminal activity has the right to know that the state has the possibility of taking measures against its subjects under certain circumstances, including, for example, the invasion of their privacy. Our suspect does not have the right to know, however, that he is the subject of technical surveillance – a right that would, of course, in any case make the technical surveillance rather futile! The Court has said:

> _The requirement of foreseeability cannot mean that an individual should be able to foresee when the authorities are likely to intercept his communications so that he can adapt his conduct accordingly. Nevertheless, the law must be sufficiently clear in its terms to give citizens an adequate indication as to the circumstances in which and conditions on which the police are empowered to resort to this secret and potentially dangerous measure. (Malone v. UK (1984) 7 EHRR 14)_

In broad terms, this has been taken to mean that a public authority may need to divulge its strategy, but need not reveal its tactics.

In a civil context, the citizen has an equal right to know how his rights will be protected. Suppose, for example, that he appeals against a housing decision by the local authority. He will want to know that the appeals process is a fair, thorough and effective one, and that it will not go on indefinitely. This means that it must be based upon law or its equivalent – a set of clear and comprehensive policies that will in practice be followed.

Accountability

The prerequisites for a proper system of accountability include a comprehensive, thorough and dynamic process of decision making and its recording. If human rights are to be properly protected there must be adequate and effective remedies against abuse, before, during or after the action of the public authority.

Necessity

Before any (qualified) human right is violated, the alternative means of obtaining the same outcome without breaching human rights should be explored and exploited. Violation of a qualified right is a last resort when no alternative means to obtain the same result is available. Necessity and proportionality are closely linked. Necessity means that the violation must be carried out, because there is no alternative, but does not describe its extent. Proportionality refers to the quality and extent of the proposed violation.

For example, let us suppose that an employer can justify violating the privacy of his employees in regard to their telephone conversations at work, because the company needs to monitor the quality of the professional advice thereby offered. However, this does not mean that the company has the right to monitor all of the telephone calls of all of its employees, for all of their duration. It may be possible to achieve the monitoring of the quality of advice offered by lesser means, and unnecessary action is usually best avoided.

Necessary, or necessary in a democratic society?

There is some possibility for confusion here, which we need to clarify. We have used 'necessary' as the word is used in everyday life and without additional phrasing. However, you will have noticed in reading through the articles 8, 9, 10 and 11 that they all make use of the same phrase: 'necessary in a democratic society'. This extends the meaning of necessary in the following way.

Freedom of thought, expression and assembly are particularly important to a functioning democracy. That democracy should be sufficiently robust to be able to cope with a certain level of dissent and disagreement. Indeed, it should welcome a healthy exchange of views, rather than the imposition of a stifling conformity. Hence, if these rights are to be interfered with, that interference must be necessary in a democratically minded society, and not an authoritarian one. The onus is on the society to tolerate the freedom in question unless it can be shown to lead to destructive consequences, as specified. That is what is meant by necessary in a democratic society.

Proportionality

The word 'proportionality' is not used in the text of the ECHR, although we come across it in the case law. It is the key factor in many judgements as to whether or not rights were breached, and in general we would say that proportionality is the key to human rights. As Starmer puts it in the most comprehensive and useful detailed guide to human rights that we have yet discovered (Starmer, 1999, p 169): 'Inherent in the whole Convention is the need to find a fair balance between the protection of individual rights and the interests of the community at large.'

The importance of establishing this fair balance is emphasized in the White Paper, *Rights Brought Home,* in which it is stated that British judges will have much to contribute to European jurisprudence in this area.

How are we to recognize proportionality in practice? The word is used in the same general sense as in everyday speech, and what is meant is an exercise in judgement that is appropriate in the circumstances.

We may start by establishing what is clearly disproportionate. For example, a surgeon does not need to remove a leg in order to correct an ingrowing toenail. Let us keep this in mind as we consider more subtle challenges to the definition of proportionality.

The German constitutional law upon which the Strasbourg judges have drawn tells us that administrative or legal power must be exercised in a way that is suitable to achieve the purpose intended and for which the power was conferred. It must not be used to a greater extent than is necessary to achieve that legitimate purpose. And finally, the exercise of the power must not impose burdens or cause harm to other legitimate interests that are disproportionate to the importance of the object to be achieved.

Telephone interception

Let us go back to our person, A, who is contemplating criminal activity. The CID wishes to prevent this, and has therefore decided, in the absence of other methods to achieve its goal, that it is necessary to monitor A's telephone conversations in the hope that these may reveal useful information.

Fair enough, we say: this policy sounds both necessary and proportionate. Provided that it is based in law and that the process is accountable, it is compliant with human rights. However, let us suppose that the CID does not intend to restrict its attention to the telephone conversations of A alone, but wants to widen the net. A regularly calls B, C, D and E, who in turn call a number of other people.

Could this extended network contain information about A's intentions which might be of use to the CID in developing a case against A? Could it be that B, C, D and E and their further conversationalists are less surveillance conscious than A, and therefore more likely to reveal something useful? Might they, while innocent themselves, unwittingly reveal A's plans to the official interceptors, who know what they are looking for?

And while the CID is about it, why does it not extend its monitoring programme to include the telephone calls of A's wife, children, mistress and extended family, who by the same logic may have something to contribute to the inquiry?

What ifs, mights and maybes of this kind may be extremely plausible, but the measures suggested are clearly outside the parameters of proportionality. If A is the suspected director of an extended criminal network, the activities of which cause massive harm – the importation of heroin on a major scale springs to mind, but there are many other examples – then the importance of the object to be achieved may justify a wider violation of human rights in its achievement. Such a case, however, would need to be argued for on its merits, and to rest upon evidence of some sort, rather than mere supposition or hope.

Prisoners' mail

We believe that the best way to understand proportionality is to practise it. Here is another application.

Let us suppose that you are a prison governor who is legally empowered to have incoming mail searched in order to prevent prohibited substances from entering your jail. An increasing amount of illegal material is entering the jail, and you want to stop this happening. In order to achieve this legal and desirable end, you decide to have all mail searched. That will achieve your objective of finding contraband items, or at least deterring their postage. It will be fair, in that you have not singled out any particular prisoner for special treatment. Finally, such a policy is administratively convenient. It can be easily monitored for its effectiveness, and it will be financially desirable compared with other policies.

A prisoner objects to his incoming mail being searched, claiming it to be an unjustified invasion of privacy. He has no record of having received prohibited materials through the post. Does he have a case?

Comment

He does. In a similar real life case, such a policy was found to be disproportionate, in that it went further than was necessary to achieve the governor's legitimate objective. In the court's opinion, the prison governor should have set out to determine which mail was most likely to contain contraband material, and to have searched that mail only.

To someone unfamiliar with the workings of the doctrine of proportionality, the judgement in this case may at first sight appear a little bizarre. Nevertheless, it is a good example of the principle in practice. Searching prisoners' mail is allowed for in the regulations, which (let us suppose) are available both to those who send and receive that mail. Therefore, the principle of legality is satisfied.

Necessity is satisfied, in that it is hard to imagine how to discover contraband material without opening the post in which it may be concealed. (Game theorists, detectives and real prison governors will already be considering what to do if contraband items should be discovered. Should they be confiscated, or allowed to reach their destination apparently unfound, in order to be used as the basis for a further intelligence operation? There are some tricky moral, legal and operational decisions ahead there, and we shall concentrate upon our original dilemma.)

However, in order to satisfy proportionality the search needs to be restricted. This is clearly not an easy solution, at least as far as the prison authorities are concerned, and one can imagine the practical difficulties that may arise. It will present the governor and his staff, we presume, with an intelligence problem that they might otherwise have avoided. But what is the alternative? Even – perhaps especially – prisoners have rights, and the alternative is to punish the innocent with the guilty.

We might suppose that this is not a very great invasion of privacy, and that any experienced prisoner is in any case going to expect the incoming mail to be subject to scrutiny, especially as outgoing mail may be censored; but those are not the primary considerations of the Court. Strasbourg does not favour blanket solutions. Its judges believe that any interference with human rights should be limited in space, finite in time and specific in tactics. We can illustrate the principle further by means of another example.

Violence at a demonstration

Suppose that an innocent bystander at a predominantly peaceful demonstration is stabbed to death by thugs who enjoy violence for its own sake, and have taken advantage of the situation to wreak havoc. Should the demonstration have been banned, because this was a possibility?

Comment

We think not. The right to peaceful demonstration is an important one, and it would be disproportionate to have banned a demonstration simply because there existed the possibility of violence.

Indeed, one wonders how many demonstrations would then in fact occur, for there would be a temptation on the part of the authorities to ban or severely restrict many of them, especially if malicious threats of disruption were made in order to achieve a ban. A blanket ban on demonstrations under such conditions would constitute a threat to the 'very essence' of the right or rights in question, against which Strasbourg has spoken out.

If it could be shown that the police had acted negligently in failing to prevent the stabbing, for example by failing to pay attention to clear and significant warnings that it was going to occur, then that is another matter. It is not an argument for banning the demonstration, however, but a case for policing it more effectively, for example by maintaining a proper intelligence system and being forewarned of trouble in time to take action to prevent it by whatever were the most appropriate and least restrictive means.

Having now considered proportionality in three examples, we shall leave it to be absorbed in practice throughout the rest of the book. We finish here with two comments. Firstly, the exercise of proportionality is not an exact science, but a matter of judgement, professional or otherwise. Moreover, what we are describing is something that in many cases may come naturally, but not be recognized under that name. Sensible managers are already applying the principle of proportionality, although they may not call it that.

Secondly, proportionality is a sub-set of reasonableness, a very familiar concept in English jurisprudence. For example, let us suppose that violence occurs at a demonstration, and the question arises as to whether or not it would have been a legitimate exercise in proportionality to have banned the event in order to have prevented this from happening. Were the actions of the police reasonable in *not* banning the demonstration, on the basis of what they knew at the time? Was their decision reasonable in the circumstances?

A HUMAN RIGHTS FLOW CHART

We shall present a relatively simple flow chart, on the basis that anything more complicated is likely to destroy its overall purpose, which is to help hard-pressed people to make both timely and sensible decisions. Individual managers, however, will wish to customize it for themselves.

The manager needs to ask himself, in any situation where human rights may arise and where there may be a question of culpability:

▮ Are there any human rights involved here?

▮ If so, are they absolute or qualified?

▮ If the right is absolute, what is the action that I need to take in order to stop the right from being violated, or to respect it as a right?

▮ If the right is qualified, and I am considering interfering with it, then:

  – What is the reason as quoted in HRA that could be used to justify my action, in general terms?

  – Where is the basis in law or procedure, for my contemplated action?

  – What alternative courses of action have I considered, in order to achieve my desired outcome – and which do *not* interfere with human rights? Why have I rejected those alternatives? And where have I recorded my decision, including some note of the alternatives that I reviewed and discarded?

– Is the course of action that I have chosen likely to achieve what is intended? Does it stop there? Will it cause any collateral damage? Are there any wider considerations that work in favour of interference in this case, in terms of protecting the rights and freedoms of others? Could I put forward a good argument for my action under cross-examination in a court of law?

Such a flow chart, if taken too seriously, may force our over-stressed manager to go on leave immediately, or suddenly thrust responsibility upon his bemused deputy! We hope, however, that such is not the case. Human rights are not intended to impede action, but to make sure that it is based upon clear and fair reasoning which works toward the general good, and which we should wish to see put into practice for ourselves.

QUESTIONS

1. Give one example of an absolute right under ECHR.

2. Which are the classic four qualified rights? (Please list them by number. If you can remember the headings, so much the better.)

3. Please give at least three reasons as to why a public authority may wish to interfere with these four rights, which could be justified under human rights doctrine.

True or false?

4. If an interference with a human right is necessary, it must also be proportionate.

5. Proportionality tends to work against blanket restrictions.

Case studies

6. You are the managing director of a small company making secret telecommunications devices for the Ministry of Defence. In order to ensure the security of your product, you carry out a rigorous screening programme of all potential employees and impose a range of other security measures that would not be found in other factories making products for the open market. Are there any potential human rights issues here, and if so, what are they?

7. Your company policy is to monitor the e-mail messages of all employees on a random basis, in order to find out what is going on and whether or not some employees are carrying out private business at work. Are there any potential human rights issues here, and if so, what are they?

8. The government has banned the movement of all livestock in order to contain an outbreak of foot-and-mouth disease that has potentially disastrous consequences. Is this a proportionate use of its legal powers?

ANSWERS

1. *Give one example of an absolute right under ECHR.*
   Article 3. Articles 4.1, 7 and 9.1.

2. *Which are the classic four qualified rights?*
   Articles 8, 9.2, 10 and 11. The right to privacy. The rights to freedom of thought, expression and assembly.

3. *Give at least three reasons as to why a public authority may wish to interfere with these four rights, which could be justified under human rights doctrine.*
   There is a wide range of choices here, including:

   - the protection of the rights and freedoms of others;

   - the economic well being of the country;

- the prevention of disorder or crime;

- the protection of health or morals;

- the protection of public order;

- territorial integrity;

- national security;

- public safety.

Note that each right has differing conditions attached to it, and that Article 10 offers additional reasons.

4. *If an interference with a human right is necessary, it must also be proportionate.*

    In our interpretation, this statement is false. 'Do we need to do this at all?' is not the same as asking: 'To what extent do we need to do it?' An investigative agency may decide that it is necessary to invade someone's freedom, but there is still the question of how far to go in doing so. However, if we take the phrase 'necessary in a democratic society' we place a wider meaning on the word 'necessary', and it could then be argued that necessity and proportionality are not separate stages in an algorithm, but two aspects of the same broad question. We remain with the view that necessity does not guarantee proportionality.

5. *Proportionality tends to work against blanket restrictions.*

    True. Blanket restrictions – all communication must cease; the whole school is gated until further notice – are often disproportionate.

6. *You are the managing director of a small company making secret telecommunications devices for the Ministry of Defence. In order to ensure the security of your product, you carry out a rigorous screening programme of all potential employees and impose a range*

of other security measures that would not be found in other factories making products for the open market. Are there any potential human rights issues here, and if so, what are they?

Questions 6 and 7 are open, and there are a huge number of potential human rights issues that could be raised in such situations. Here are some general thoughts on 6:

– Does your contract specify that security vetting is necessary?

– Are you a public authority, and thereby bound to observe human rights? It sounds as if you might be a hybrid authority. Any court would need to take note of any human rights issues that came to its attention, whatever the official status of your company. However, as a public authority you have a positive obligation to uphold human rights – which is a greater obligation than simply to be prepared to answer for their violation.

– Screening and other security measures could affect employees' right to privacy, including their family life. They might also affect their rights under Articles 9, 10 and 11. It would be necessary to show that your security policies are both necessary and proportionate in order to protect what needs to be protected, but no more. They must in addition be accessible, and you must be able to demonstrate that they are followed properly, for example with due regard to any safeguards built in, such as any right of appeal. Finally, your policies must not be discriminatory in regard to the right to family life, or any other declared right.

7. *Your company policy is to monitor the e-mail messages of all employees on a random basis, in order to find out what is going on and whether or not some employees are carrying out private business at work. Are there any potential human rights issues here, and if so, what are they?*

There is some resemblance to the previous question:

- There is the issue of your status as a private organization or public authority.

- Whatever your policies are, they need to be recorded, and clearly and accessibly communicated to those whom they will affect.

- The issue of the proportionality of the company's policy on e-mail is highly relevant. It is not necessarily wrong to read e-mail, nor to do so on a random basis. After all, privacy is a qualified right. People do not have a total expectation of privacy at work, and they should in any case have been warned of company policy in this area.

- The company needs to give some thought to the logic of its policy. Why is it reading *these* e-mails? 'In order to find out what is going on' sounds a very loose phrase. And what about the issue of private business at work? What is meant by private business? Is the company saying that any private e-mail is a violation of company policy, to be followed by a specified penalty? Or is there some room for manoeuvre here? If so, who decides, and on what basis? We suggest that a sensible company policy will be sufficiently clear to let people know where they stand, while at the same time allowing managers to interpret it in the spirit in which it is intended.

- Finally, there is legislation in this area, and you will need to consider whether or not the Regulation of Investigatory Powers Act applies.

8. *The government has banned the movement of all livestock in order to contain an outbreak of foot-and-mouth disease that has potentially disastrous consequences. Is this a proportionate use of its legal powers?*

   As we write this text in north Devon in the spring of 2001 we are in the middle of a disastrous foot-and-mouth outbreak, which is having an immensely damaging effect on the rural economy both locally and nationally. As we cannot yet know either the course of the disease or the efficacy of the government's counter-measures, we are tempted to say that only posterity can judge the proportionality of the government's measures. However, we can make some general comments:

- The example given of a counter-measure is of a ban on the movement of livestock. We might argue that this is within the parameters of proportionality in that its effect is mainly limited, we presume, to the farming and haulage industries. Other measures, such as banning the use of footpaths, have also been put in place by the government. We could argue these to be less proportionate, as their effects are and will be felt by everyone who might wish to use the countryside. Moreover, they are having a crippling effect on tourism, which was not their intention. This is clearly a disproportionate outcome. Moreover, tourism is a greater source of revenue than farming, so that the overall justification for the violation of human rights – to protect the economy – may be invalid.

- In general terms, however, the proportionality of any counter-measures to foot-and-mouth must be judged against the nature and extent of the threat posed by the disease itself. In this case, the threat is in the area of the economic well being of the country. This justifies the possibility of draconian counter-measures, provided always that they are likely to achieve the outcome for which they are intended. The government's agencies would need to argue, if challenged in court, that the counter-measures imposed were necessary for the main objective of tackling foot-and-mouth, and their secondary consequences could not have been avoided. It would also be wise to indicate, as the government has done, that measures have been put in place to help those affected.

- The application of proportionality is not an exact science. Experts as well as lay people may disagree as to how foot-

and-mouth should be dealt with, and the proper place for debating the broader political issues is in the political arena and not the courtroom. It is not up to the judges to say what should be done about foot-and-mouth. They may have a role to play, however, in reviewing the legality, necessity and proportionality of such measures as are adopted, whether by the appeal of a victim for a breach of human rights, or an application for judicial review of the decisions leading to such an outcome.

– At the moment we cannot say, however, that there is an obvious breach of human rights on which to mount a case. Animals have no human rights. Footpath users have no right to roam, under either ECHR or common law. Nor is there an obvious right to which the tourist industry can appeal, should it wish to claim that the measures taken to curb foot-and-mouth have been disproportionate in their effects, however arguable this claim may be, on its merits. They may indeed be the victims of the policy, but what is the right that has been violated? We await developments with interest!

5

The right to life

EUROPEAN CONVENTION ON HUMAN RIGHTS, ARTICLE 2

1. Everyone's right to life shall be protected by law. No one shall be deprived of his life intentionally save in the execution of a sentence of a court following his conviction of a crime for which this penalty is provided by law.

2. Deprivation of life shall not be regarded as inflicted in contravention of this article when it results from the use of force which is no more than absolutely necessary:

   (a) in defence of any person from unlawful violence;

   (b) in order to effect a lawful arrest or to prevent the escape of a person lawfully detained;

   (c) in action lawfully taken for the purpose of quelling a riot or insurrection.

Commentary

The right to life is clearly the most important right under the Convention, since without life all other rights are meaningless. Nevertheless it is a restricted right, for in reality no state can guarantee life itself. It can only offer a guarantee that its agents will not take life arbitrarily or unnecessarily, and recognize that they have some obligation to protect life against clear threat. That, however, is important enough. When might the state take life? On the whole, when exercising force, and hence the structure of the Article, which is in reality concerned about the legitimate and proportionate use of force. The police and prison service, which are both public services, are traditionally ascribed a monopoly on the use of legitimate force within the UK, and this Article applies primarily to them. However, we may also need to apply it to other agencies carrying out police or prison-type work. There has been an enormous growth in the private security industry over the past 20 years, and there are now reported to be more private security employees than police officers in the UK. Similarly, there has been the development of private prisons.

Unlike in some other countries, the issuing of firearms has been restricted to the police; but the use of firearms is not the only way of taking life. We would therefore suggest that, while Article 2 applies primarily to the police, other agencies might be affected by it when acting as public authorities. With that proviso in mind, we shall confine our comments on this vital but restricted article to points of general relevance.

NON-LETHAL ALTERNATIVES TO THE USE OF DEADLY FORCE

Article 2 of the Convention does not define situations where it is permissible intentionally to kill an individual. It defines situations where it is permissible to use force that may result, as the unintended outcome of the use of that force, in deprivation of life. Thus, if there is an alternative to the use of lethal force that is known to be effective in achieving the purpose for which lethal force would have been used, that non-lethal alternative should be chosen.

Let us suppose that an armed robber is intending to shoot a bank teller, and the police armed response unit is in a position, in the laconic jargon that springs to the tongue of law enforcement officials in such circumstances, to 'take him out'. Under common law, the use of lethal force in such a situation might be assessed as reasonable to prevent the crime, and thus lawful. However, if we apply Article 2 in this situation, the police officer has to ask himself, not whether or not his contemplated action would be regarded as reasonable under the circumstances, but whether or not it is limited to what is no more than is absolutely necessary to achieve his lawful objective. If he can prevent unlawful violence by non-lethal force, then that is the option he should choose. How is he to make that decision? Strasbourg does not provide a formula, but has stated that in establishing whether or not the use of force was 'strictly proportionate' regard must be had to the nature of the aim pursued; the dangers to life and limb of innocent parties, inherent in the situation; and the degree of the risk that the force employed might result in loss of life.

OPERATIONAL COMMAND AND CONTROL

In a number of cases the European Court of Human Rights has gone beyond the examination of the judgement of the person who actually pulled the trigger, to consider how the operation as a whole was planned and controlled, and here we shall illustrate our analysis with a British case.

McCann and Others v. the United Kingdom (1995)

This triple shooting aroused great interest, and was examined first by the European Commission and then by the Court itself, sitting as a Grand Chamber of 17 members.

Three IRA members were shot dead by an SAS unit in Gibraltar, who believed that they were about to detonate a bomb. In the event that belief proved mistaken. There was no bomb ready to be detonated, and the terrorists were not armed at the time they were shot.

In determining if the use of force was compatible with Article 2, the Court had to scrutinize not only if the force used by the soldiers was strictly in proportion to the legitimate aim of protecting persons against unlawful violence, but also if the anti-terrorist operation was planned and controlled by the authorities so as to minimize, to the greatest extent possible, recourse to lethal force.

In considering the actions of the soldiers the Court accepted that they honestly believed, in the light of the information they were given, that it was necessary to shoot the suspects in order to prevent them from detonating a bomb and causing loss of life. It pronounced that the use of force may be justified where it is based on an honest belief perceived to be valid at the time, but which subsequently turns out to be mistaken. The Court decided that the actions of the soldiers themselves did not constitute a violation of Article 2 of the Convention.

However, that decision did not complete the Court's judgement. They went on to examine the command and control of the operation, and decided that it was flawed. A series of working hypotheses were conveyed to the four soldiers as certainties, thereby making the use of lethal force almost inevitable, especially as the soldiers in question were highly trained in its use.

In sum, having regard to:

- the decision not to prevent the suspects from travelling into Gibraltar;

- the failure of the authorities to make sufficient allowances for the possibility that their intelligence assessments might, in some respects at least, be erroneous; and

- the automatic recourse to lethal force when the soldiers opened fire;

the Court was not persuaded that the killing of the three terrorists constituted the use of force that was no more than absolutely necessary in defence of persons from unlawful violence. Accordingly, it found that there had been a breach of Article 2 of the Convention by the UK.

Commentary

We have included this summary for three reasons:

1. It illustrates the wider considerations that the ECtHR is capable of bringing to the examination of the use of lethal force under the doctrine of proportionality, in determining the liability of a member state.

2. It demonstrates, in our view, an objective, fair-minded and sensible judgement by the ECtHR.

3. It is evidence, if evidence were needed, against the presumption (still held by some sections of the British press) that the ECtHR is an officious and meddlesome creation to which no true Briton should give any credence. This is a doubly fallacious view. As we have seen, the UK played a major role in creating the ECHR in 1950; 1995 was therefore a little late to object to its application. Secondly, the ECtHR sees its role as to correct future national behaviour in a practical way, rather than punish past individual mistakes, and we may see the McCann case as an illustration of this. This is not an officious and meddlesome institution, but a necessary means for the establishment and protection of fundamental rights, in sometimes very difficult situations.

THE OBLIGATION ON A PUBLIC AUTHORITY TO PROTECT LIFE

Article 2 of ECHR cannot be read as imposing an absolute obligation upon the state to protect life, whatever the circumstances. As we have already pointed out, Article 2 does not actually give a right to life as such. Rather, the Convention imposes a positive obligation upon each member state to uphold human rights, including the right to life. What does this mean in practice, for public authorities in particular? How do we decide the parameters of the obligation that this imposes upon public authorities? As with other legal or quasi-legal questions, rather than speculate we should turn to the relevant case law. Here is a case that makes a number of points, and is well worth attention.

Osman v. the United Kingdom (1998)

In this case Mr Paul Paget-Lewis, a deranged schoolteacher, shot dead the father of a pupil about whom he had formed an obsession, and wounded the boy himself. The widow attempted to obtain domestic redress and then took her case to the ECtHR, claiming breaches of a number of articles, including the right to life and the right to a fair trial – about which we shall say more later.

Article 2

In regard to Article 2, Mrs Osman's argument was that Paul Paget-Lewis was known to be an unstable and dangerous person and had made his obsession with her son very clear, before the fatal attack. She argued that the Metropolitan Police had not done enough to protect her family against a known and serious threat to life, and that they could and should have prevented what happened.

The ECtHR recognized that she had a case. Article 2 of the Convention may imply in certain well-defined circumstances a positive obligation on the authorities to take preventative measures to protect an individual whose life is at risk from the criminal acts of another individual.

However, the obligation to protect life must be interpreted in a way that does not impose an impossible or disproportionate burden on the authorities. Accordingly, not every claimed risk to life can entail for the authorities a Convention requirement to take operational measures to prevent that risk from materializing.

The need to respect one article cannot be used to justify the violation of another. There is a need to ensure that the police exercise their powers to control and prevent crime in a manner that fully respects the due process and other guarantees that legitimately place restraints on the scope of their action to investigate crime and bring offenders to justice. These restraints include the guarantees contained in Articles 5 and 8 of the Convention. In other words, the state in this case could not simply lock up Paul Paget-Lewis because he was believed to constitute a threat, nor take other measures against him that unjustifiably breached his rights to liberty and privacy.

In the view of the Court in this case, the applicants had failed to point to any decisive stage in the sequence of the events leading up to the tragic shooting when it could be said that the police knew or ought to have known that the lives of the Osman family were at real and immediate risk from Paget-Lewis. The applicants had pointed to a series of missed opportunities that would have enabled the police to neutralize the threat posed by Paget-Lewis. But it could not be said that these measures, judged reasonably, would in fact have produced that result or that a domestic court would have convicted him or ordered his detention in a psychiatric hospital on the basis of the evidence adduced before it.

The Court had already noted that the police must discharge their duties in a manner that is compatible with the rights and freedoms of individuals. In the circumstances of this case, they could not be criticized for attaching weight to the presumption of innocence or failing to use powers of arrest, search and seizure. The Court gave regard to the police's reasonably held view that they lacked, at relevant times, the required standard of suspicion to use those powers. Moreover, the police disputed that any action taken would in fact have produced concrete results.

For these reasons, the Court concluded that there had been no violation of Article 2.

Article 6 and public interest immunity

Article 6 guarantees the right to a fair hearing, which Mrs Osman claimed that she had been denied. She had wished to sue the Metropolitan Police for negligence in failing to protect her family. They had refused to provide the evidence that would have established whether or not they could be judged to have been negligent, and consequently she could not have a fair trial because relevant evidence would be withheld.

The police had claimed that it was not in the public interest that they account for their actions in regard to the threat to the Osman family, as under English law they were immune as a public service from being required to produce such an account. This is the so-called 'defence of public interest immunity', which we need to examine a little further.

Public interest immunity is the doctrine that a public service does not have to account for its actions in detail, for the very practical reason that if it did face such an obligation it would be unable to concentrate its resources upon its proper role. It would not be in the public interest, for example, for a police service to be so completely preoccupied with accounting for its previous alleged mistakes that it lacked the resources to concentrate upon preventing future crimes.

The Court examined this doctrine and applied to it the principle of proportionality. It recognized that the reasons for this exclusionary rule to protect the police from negligence actions are based on the view that the interests of the community as a whole are best served by a police service whose efficiency and effectiveness in the battle against crime is not jeopardized by the constant risk of exposure to tortious liability for policy and operational decisions.

In the present case, however, the (English) Court of Appeal proceeded on the basis that the rule provided a watertight defence to the police. It was impossible to prise open an immunity that the police enjoyed from civil suit in respect of their acts and omissions in the investigation and suppression of crime.

The Court observed that the application of the rule in this manner without further enquiry into the existence of competing public interest considerations confers a blanket immunity on the police for their acts and omissions during the investigation and suppression of crime, and amounts to an unjustifiable restriction on an applicant's right to have a determination on the merits of his claim against the police in deserving cases.

In its view, it must be open to a domestic court to have regard to the presence of other public interest considerations, which pull in the opposite direction to the application of the rule. Failing this, there will be no distinction made between degrees of negligence or of harm suffered or any consideration of the justice of a particular case. Furthermore, the applicants' case involved the alleged failure to protect the life of a child and their view that that failure was the result of a catalogue of acts and omissions that amounted to grave negligence as opposed to minor acts of incompetence. The applicants also claimed that the police had assumed responsibility for their safety. Finally, the harm sustained was of the most serious nature.

The conclusion of the Court was clear. Mrs Osman deserved her day in court, and had not had it. There had been a violation of Article 6.

Comment

By inference, the police (or any other public authority that might have wished to plead the same argument) can no longer rely upon the blanket defence of public interest immunity in regard to an allegation of a breach of human rights. The authority has an obligation not only to uphold human rights but also to be prepared to account for its actions or inactions in doing so.

THE LIMITATIONS OF ARTICLE 2

ECHR cannot resolve all the controversies that arise in regard to the right to life and other fundamental issues. Here we shall briefly mention just a few issues out of the many that might be raised.

Abortion

Does a foetus have a right to life, and, if so, is that right an absolute one? In *Patton v. the United Kingdom* (1980) the applicant alleged a breach of Article 2 (and other rights) because his estranged wife obtained an abortion despite his opposition. The Commission decided that, as a matter of construction of the Convention, the right to life could apply only to those who have already been born. It had three options in regard to the possible extension of this construction:

1. to exclude the foetus from the right to life altogether;

2. to grant it an absolute protection; or

3. to grant it a limited protection.

Option 2 was rapidly excluded, since in practice this could remove the right to life of the mother. Where should the Commission go from there? It did not feel itself ready to decide. In an area of such sensitivity, and in the absence of any clear consensus within Europe, either moral, legal or religious, as to what should happen about abortion, the Commission was not prepared to make a general ruling on this subject, although it did not rule out option 3 as a future possibility. The Commission took its deliberations no further than to decide that in this case there had been no breach of Article 2. The decision about whether or under what circumstances to allow abortion should be left to each member state, as it fell within its 'margin of appreciation' – a term we explore elsewhere.

Siamese or conjoined twins

In a recent (2000) case in which the UK was the subject of international publicity, parents, medical services and the courts faced a tragic dilemma. Two little girls had been born as Siamese twins. Medical opinion had it that if the situation were left alone both would die within months. If, on the other hand, doctors intervened to attempt to save the life of the stronger child, the weaker would inevitably die. This was a moral and legal dilemma for which human rights did not offer a solution, although Article 2 was taken into account in the deliberations of the judges. In the end, however, they stated that HRA added nothing to the common law in addressing this case. Both twins had the right to life, and it was irrelevant, for human rights purposes, to consider how long that life might last or what would be its quality. They had no right to take one life to save another, and the purpose of the operation could not therefore be construed in those terms.

The right to die

There is no right to die under ECHR, and patients may be kept alive by advances in medicine by which they might not have chosen to benefit, were the choice in reality theirs to make. Human rights are in essence concerned with human dignity, and people should always be treated with dignity and respect, as the UDHR proclaims. However, that general proclamation does not tell the hard-pressed doctor what to do, if he has the option of keeping alive a patient who will then enjoy a very inferior quality of life, and who might, as a rational person, have chosen to die under such circumstances if able to make the choice.

Medical responsibilities, it has been argued, are greatly increased under the HRA, and we would urge those of our readers who are professionally involved in this area to treat this book as a stimulus to gaining further and more detailed knowledge. Not only doctors but also health service managers need to be aware of their changing responsibilities here.

Euthanasia

ECHR does not forbid 'passive' euthanasia, but 'active' euthanasia would be difficult to reconcile with it. In other words, it may be possible, notwithstanding Article 2 and its obligations, to allow a patient to die when medical intervention might have saved his life. Active intervention by a doctor to bring that life to an end is, however, quite another matter – even if it is claimed that the patient consented.

The proper allocation of medical resources

The proper allocation of medical resources is something that has concerned doctors from Hippocrates onwards. Human rights now need to be woven into the decision-making process. Let us suppose that you are a doctor and have a limited supply of an extremely expensive medicine at your disposal. This medicine can achieve dramatic curative results. You have two patients who would both, as far as you can judge, respond positively to treatment with the new medicine, but you do not have enough medicine to treat them both. If A receives the medicine, then she may recover, but in the meantime B will probably die, and vice versa. To whom should you give the medicine, or rather, how should you make the choice between A and B?

There is a variety of criteria under which such a choice could be made, and a good deal of medical ethics is concerned with helping doctors and other medical professionals to make fair and defensible decisions in such challenging circumstances.

However, there is still a choice to be made. Is further information relevant? Let us take it as given that A is a middle-aged woman with a stable and happy home life. She has a devoted husband and a number of children. She works part-time as a medical receptionist and is actively involved in the community. She has a strong religious conviction. She is content to accept the decision of the medical profession as to what treatment she should receive for her disease which, in the absence of radical new treatment, is almost certain to lead to her death within months. If she receives the treatment, she will probably, in the opinion of her doctor, benefit strongly from it in terms of her likelihood of recovery.

B is a middle-aged woman with a history of confused and unhappy relationships. She currently lives alone and is supported by the state. She is estranged from her only daughter, who is a drug addict. She has known about her potentially fatal disease for some time, but her mental attitude has been far from positive, and she has not, in the opinion of her doctor, done the right things to combat it. At the same time he suspects that she would be bitterly resentful if she were to learn that a possible treatment had been withheld in favour of another. She is judged less likely than A to respond well to the treatment.

Let us take the last factor mentioned in both cases as the one that might, in fact, most strongly influence medical opinion in terms of making the necessary decision about the allocation of the new drug. On the basis of which patient is more likely to benefit, we choose A.

What is the position here in regard to human rights? A difficult one, as both patients have the right to life, and rights are equal, universal and inalienable. Under that logic, a doctor would have difficulty in claiming that he is justified in allocating resources according to where they will do the most good, if in the process of so doing he deprives some patients of care that they might otherwise have received. (We suppose that there may be a difference between taking something away from someone and deciding not to offer it in the first place, but we should need to see how such an argument might work out in court.)

How is the medical profession to resolve this dilemma? We suppose that it will not do so alone. Grievances will be raised and examined in court, and the common law will presumably develop accordingly. The passage of the HRA does not create additional medical resources, and where demand exceeds supply decisions about rationing will always have to be made, whatever the position of the decision maker under human rights.

However, the framework for decision making that human rights bring with them may be of partial assistance in the examination of such dilemmas. Even if those principles do not resolve the irresolvable, at least they offer a framework for decision making that can be shared by both doctors and lawyers and, we would argue, is equally accessible to the informed lay person.

QUESTIONS

True or false?

1. Article 2 of the HRA gives the police the absolute right to shoot rioters, fugitives from justice, and anyone resisting lawful arrest.

2. Public authorities do not have to defend their decisions in court, even if the consequences of those decisions, it could be argued, have included a loss of life that could have been prevented.

3. Under the HRA, any form of abortion will be declared illegal.

4. Any doctor who fails to exert himself to the utmost in order to save a patient's life, is thereby guilty of a breach of Article 2.

5. The doctrine of proportionality cannot be applied in the context of the right to life.

6. The result of the Osman case was that the Metropolitan Police were found guilty of breaching the right to life.

7. The result of the McCann case was that the British Army was found guilty of having breached Article 3 of ECHR.

ANSWERS

1. *Article 2 of the HRA gives the police the absolute right to shoot rioters, fugitives from justice, and anyone resisting lawful arrest.*
   False. This is a complete misreading of the article in question.

2. _Public authorities do not have to defend their decisions in court, even if the consequences of those decisions, it could be argued, have included a loss of life that could have been prevented._

   False. The defence here is that of public interest immunity, which is questioned under Osman.

3. _Under the HRA, any form of abortion will be declared illegal._

   False. Neither ECHR nor the HRA says anything on abortion. Case law does not extend the right to life to include the unborn child.

4. _Any doctor who fails to exert himself to the utmost in order to save a patient's life, is thereby guilty of a breach of Article 2._

   False. Everything depends upon the circumstances.

5. _The doctrine of proportionality cannot be applied in the context of the right to life._

   In our opinion, this statement is false. The right to life is not a qualified right, like 8, 9.2, 10 or 11, and there are no circumstances under which the state may take life in order to achieve another objective. However, if we consider Osman, the Court applied the principle of proportionality in reviewing the decisions of the police in the context of protecting life. No public authority has unlimited resources, and there will be situations in which it would be unreasonable to expect that all available resources should be devoted to protecting or saving the life of one person. As always, however, everything depends upon the circumstances!

6. _The result of the Osman case was that the Metropolitan Police were found guilty of breaching the right to life._

   False. Article 6 – the right to a fair hearing – was breached. Moreover, the word 'guilty' sits uneasily in this context. The fundamental purpose of the Court is to ensure future compliance with human rights.

7. _The result of the McCann case was that the British Army was found guilty of having breached Article 3 of ECHR._

False. A security operation conducted by a number of agencies was found to have given insufficient consideration to the alternatives to lethal resolution, and there was therefore a breach of Article 2. As in question 6, the word 'guilty' is in any case inappropriate.

6

Liberty, security and trial

ARTICLES 5 AND 6

Article 5 begins by stating that everyone has the right to liberty and security of person, and then goes on to indicate what this means in practice. Article 6 similarly states that everyone has the right to a fair trial, and then goes on to indicate the practical implications of the article.

Both articles will be of most interest to citizens when their rights in either area are threatened, either by arbitrary arrest, detention, or by an unfair trial. It is therefore most important that agencies of the state such as the police should fully comprehend their powers and responsibilities under these two articles, and exercise them properly.

Our book is not intended as a professional training manual for police officers, and we would suppose that most people do not make arrests, detain suspects and gather evidence for criminal prosecutions as a regular part of their everyday work. We would suggest, however, that many businesses have something to protect and employ some sort of security on their premises, whether that security be walls, people, cameras, or electronic security measures designed to find out who is trying to gain access to a database.

Many organizations may on occasion need to detain people, such as suspected shoplifters, or drunken patients attacking hospital staff, or angry parents attacking teachers. A working understanding of how HRA affects both previous law and customary behaviour in this area will therefore be useful to the manager, provided that it is not used as a substitute for full legal training where that may be necessary, and it is important for everyone to be clear on the broad principles upon which these two separate but overlapping articles are based.

ARTICLE 5 – RIGHT TO LIBERTY AND SECURITY

1. Everyone has the right to liberty and security of person. No one shall be deprived of his liberty save in the following cases and in accordance with a procedure prescribed by law:

   (a) the lawful detention of a person after conviction by a competent court;

   (b) the lawful arrest or detention of a person for non-compliance with the lawful order of a court or in order to secure the fulfilment of any obligation prescribed by law;

   (c) the lawful arrest or detention of a person effected for the purpose of bringing him before the competent legal authority on reasonable suspicion of having committed an offence or when it is reasonably considered necessary to prevent his committing an offence or fleeing after having done so;

   (d) the detention of a minor by lawful order for the purpose of educational supervision or his lawful detention for the purpose of bringing him before the competent legal authority;

(e) the lawful detention of persons for the prevention of the spreading of infectious diseases, of persons of unsound mind, alcoholics or drug addicts or vagrants;

(f) the lawful arrest or detention of a person to prevent his effecting an unauthorized entry into the country or of a person against whom action is being taken with a view to deportation or extradition.

2. Everyone who is arrested shall be informed promptly, in a language that he understands, of the reasons for his arrest and of any charge against him.

3. Everyone arrested or detained in accordance with the provisions of paragraph 1(c) of this Article shall be brought promptly before a judge or other officer authorized by law to exercise judicial power and shall be entitled to trial within a reasonable time or to release pending trial. Release may be conditioned by guarantees to appear for trial.

4. Everyone who is deprived of his liberty by arrest or detention shall be entitled to take proceedings by which the lawfulness of his detention shall be decided speedily by a court and his release ordered if the detention is not lawful.

5. Everyone who has been the victim of arrest or detention in contravention of the provisions of this Article shall have an enforceable right to compensation.

Commentary on Article 5 – liberty and security

Article 5 is more concerned with liberty than security, which is not defined.

There is a presumption that the citizen is entitled to liberty, and any infringement of that liberty must be justified. It must be based in law, and where the exercise of discretion is allowed for, that discretion must be exercised reasonably.

Reasonable and unreasonable suspicion

In regard to the professional use of the power to restrict liberty, the requirement of 'reasonableness' forms an essential part of the safeguard against arbitrary arrest and detention that this article provides. Having a reasonable suspicion presupposes the existence of facts or information that would satisfy an objective observer that the person concerned might have committed an offence, and not just an honest belief on the part of the person making the arrest that his action is justified.

Reasonable and unreasonable delay

Momentary deprivations of liberty are clearly a lesser infringement than greater ones; and it may be necessary to award some discretion to an authority in terms of how it goes about achieving a legitimate objective.

An obligation to submit to examination for security reasons may be permissible. However, proportionality applies here as elsewhere, and the greater the deprivation of liberty, the more it must be justified. Let us suppose, for example, that a private security company is protecting a public entertainment of some sort, and needs to restrict the liberty of those intending to attend the event, perhaps in order to search them for illegal substances, or verify their tickets.

There are no obvious grounds for objection to a legitimately occasioned deprivation of liberty. But the victim may be entitled to query its manner or duration (provided that a forum can be found for the complaint) if these are claimed to be unreasonable. Under such circumstances the company in question cannot simply assert as a complete defence that the delay was unexpected, or that the operation, for example to check for counterfeit tickets or remove unlawfully-possessed alcohol, took longer than they expected. There must be some indication of anticipation and planning for the event that would be accepted as reasonable under the circumstances.

Compensation

Article 5 states specifically that everyone who has been the victim of arrest or detention in contravention of the provisions of this Article shall have an enforceable right to compensation (Paragraph 5). It does not specify, however, how this compensation should be calculated, nor even that it should be monetary, although the word has usually, we believe, been interpreted with that meaning.

Organizations are not unnaturally keenly interested in what their mistakes will cost them – some may even wish to calculate whether or not it is 'worth' deliberately violating a right – and will wish to know how compensation is calculated.

The short answer is that Strasbourg does not tell us. Strasbourg sees itself as a tribunal and not a court. Its purpose is more to correct future behaviour than punish past mistakes, and any damages it has awarded have usually been compensatory, in the language of the experts, rather than exemplary. A jury might decide that a libel award should be exemplary. Strasbourg would not apply this notion in regard to breaches of any articles.

Strasbourg refers to the usual principles that are applied in calculating the award of compensation or damages, but fails to go on and make it clear what those principles are. We may see this absence of clarity and predictability as a breach of human rights, but there is nowhere to take our appeal beyond Strasbourg! We would advise the manager to tread cautiously in this area, and to remember that when human rights are raised as an issue in a British court it will be the court in question, and not Strasbourg, which decides the amount of compensation or other penalty that is appropriate for a breach of the article in question.

As we have stated, Articles 5 and 6 overlap to some extent. We need to be treated with dignity and respect for our human rights when we are in detention, whether or not that detention leads to a criminal charge; and we retain the same right to be treated with dignity and respect during any trial that may occur, and after its completion. In addition, we have certain specific rights that are common to both articles. Let us now go on to examine Article 6.

ARTICLE 6 – A FAIR TRIAL

1. In the determination of his civil rights and obligations or of any criminal charge against him, everyone is entitled to a fair and public hearing within a reasonable time by an independent and impartial tribunal established by law. Judgement shall be pronounced publicly but the press and public may be excluded from all or part of the trial in the interests of morals, public order or national security in a democratic society, where the interests of juveniles or the protection of the private life of the parties so require, or to the extent strictly necessary in the opinion of the court in special circumstances where publicity would prejudice the interests of justice.

2. Everyone charged with a criminal offence shall be presumed innocent until proved guilty according to law.

3. Everyone charged with a criminal offence has the following minimum rights:

    (a) to be informed promptly, in a language which he understands and in detail, of the nature and cause of the accusation against him;

    (b) to have adequate time and facilities for the preparation of his absence;

    (c) to defend himself in person or through legal assistance of his own choosing or, if he has not sufficient means to pay for legal assistance, to be given it free when the interests of justice so require;

    (d) to examine or have examined witnesses against him and to obtain the attendance and examination of witnesses on his behalf under the same conditions as witnesses against him;

(e) to have the free assistance of an interpreter if he cannot understand or speak the language used in court.

Comments

Application to all courts and legal proceedings

The article does not restrict itself to criminal trials in a criminal court of law. As it states: 'In the determination of his civil rights and obligations or of any criminal charge against him, everyone is entitled to a fair and public hearing...'. In other words, whether the trial be civil or criminal, it must consist of a fair and public hearing; and there are additional safeguards for a criminal trial.

The British government's intention is that human rights should be able to be raised and protected in any court, and HRA makes it a legal requirement that any court, as a public authority, must uphold and protect human rights.

Servants of the state

Does ECHR/HRA protect the servants of the state, such as soldiers, police officers, or civil servants? There is room for argument here.

On the one hand, absolute rights and fundamental freedoms such as freedom from torture or inhuman and degrading treatment must apply to everyone. On the other hand, Article 11.2 refers to the imposition of lawful restrictions upon the exercise of the right to freedom of assembly and association, by members of the armed forces, of the police, or of the administration of the state – and we may easily understand the need for a restriction there.

The historical position in regard to the application of Article 6 to public servants is complicated. If we judge by the European case law, it could be argued that the right to a fair trial might not always be claimed in such circumstances. We need to ask: is the process wherein the violation is claimed, a trial in the full sense? Who claims the violation?

Autonomous concepts

Strasbourg has stated that what constitutes a criminal trial is an autonomous concept. In other words, it is not simply a matter for the nation in question to determine whether or not a process is purely administrative, or a criminal hearing, which is entitled to the protection of Article 6. There are general principles that must be applied.

If A is charged with murder before a state court, then he is clearly entitled to the protection of the right to a fair trial. If, on the other hand, he has simply arrived late for work, and his employer intends to fine him, the right to a fair trial does not apply. Even in such apparently trivial circumstances, the person who seems to be at fault should at least be given the opportunity to explain his tardiness, which may have been unavoidable, or even to be commended. But this is, in broad terms, an administrative process and not a trial. Between these two extremes are the more ambiguous cases, which need to be analysed objectively.

Strasbourg will decide the status of the process according to such criteria as the seriousness of the offence that is alleged, and the extent of the penalty that could be imposed if the candidate were found to be in the wrong. Where dismissal is an option, Article 6 applies.

If a victim believes that he has a grievance based on a violation of his human rights, and is unable to raise the issue within his organization, then he needs to get it before a public court or tribunal in order to ventilate the grievance where redress may be obtained.

Features of a fair trial

ECtHR analysis suggests that Strasbourg perceives four features as being, prima facie, necessary to a fair trial:

- privilege against self-incrimination;

- equality of arms between parties;

▓ the opportunity to cross-examine witnesses;

▓ the right of the accused in criminal cases to be present at the hearing.

Self-incrimination

It is generally recognized that there is some privilege against self-incrimination in a court of law. In _Saunders v. United Kingdom_ (1996) 23 EHRR 313, the applicant had been legally obliged to answer questions put to him during an investigation by officials of the Department of Trade and Industry in connection with company fraud. The statements he had made were then used against him in his trial and conviction for false accounting, theft and conspiracy. Strasbourg found a breach of Article 6 (1).

Strasbourg has not declared an absolute right to silence in a criminal trial. When the issue of a total refusal to answer questions, and the inferences drawn therefrom, has been raised, Strasbourg has sought to determine the legality of the procedure under national law, what was appropriate in the circumstances, and whether or not the trial as a whole was fair.

Equality of arms

> _The concept of equality of arms implies that each party must be afforded a reasonable opportunity to present his case – including his evidence – under conditions that do not place him at a substantial disadvantage vis-à-vis his opponent. (Dombo Beheer BV v. The Netherlands (1993) 18 EHRR 213)_

ECtHR has not stated that both prosecution and defence must necessarily be in possession of identical information. The implication is, however, that if the defence is not given information that could be of significant value to it, then the trial is unlikely to be fair.

Detailed rules on evidence are a matter for national courts, and Strasbourg has largely confined itself to commenting upon breaches that have led to an unfair trial.

OVERALL COMMENTS

Articles 5 and 6 have led to a large number of appeals at Strasbourg, and deliberations in regard to the points raised have been both complex and subtle. This is a huge area of law and procedure. We do not wish to over-simplify the points that have arisen, nor to utter bland and potentially misleading generalizations. We would urge the manager to be aware of the following:

▓ Article 5 emphasizes the need to plan properly for events or processes that may result in the temporary infringement of liberty, and to make sure that any deliberate deprivation of liberty, where legally allowed for, is based upon the proper use of reasonable suspicion.

▓ The effect of Article 6 is that the manager should be aware that any disciplinary proceedings that may culminate in dismissal might then reach an industrial tribunal, which will be concerned about the human rights aspects of the case in point as they may be raised by the plaintiff.

▓ How proactive the management wishes to be about preventing possible human rights abuses or violations is a matter for the private company concerned. However, there are strong arguments for pre-emptive action to remedy obvious breaches and violations, and to ensure that procedures and processes are congruent with human rights-supporting principles such as timeliness and procedural fairness.

▓ The HRA should present little or no fears for the well-prepared and well-organized private company or public authority which treats its employees with dignity and respect, which is fully aware of the law in regard to employment, conditions at work and other relevant matters, and which can properly account for its actions. However, a brief but thorough human rights audit of company procedures in even the best prepared of organizations, perhaps by a third party, may prove worthwhile. As the military maxim states, time spent in reconnaissance is seldom wasted. A human rights audit, like a positive vetting process, is limited to exposing obvious historical or contemporary faults, mistakes and weaknesses, and cannot give the whole picture. It is, nevertheless, an indispensable beginning to the creation of a sound human rights culture within any organization.

Auditing will need to cover both what is supposed to happen and what happens in reality, and in any real organization there is bound to be some gap between the two, as well as an absence, in some areas, of any written or generally understood policy at all.

QUESTIONS

True or false?

1. Under ECHR case law on Article 5, reasonable suspicion can be taken to mean suspicion that would satisfy an objective observer, that a deprivation of liberty was necessary.

2. Strasbourg has not declared an absolute right to silence for the accused in a criminal trial.

3. The protection of Article 6 applies to civil as well as criminal trials.

4. Strasbourg guarantees the right to trial by jury.

5. The ECHR does not apply to servants of the state such as police officers, soldiers or civil servants.

6. Suppose an illegal immigrant has been put on trial for murder, but cannot understand the language of the court. Is he entitled to the free services of an interpreter – even if the case is very strong against him?

7. The press may never be excluded from a fair trial.

Case studies

8. One of your teachers has been assaulted by an angry parent, whom you have detained by locking him in the storeroom until the police arrive. He is pounding on the locked door, shouting that his rights have been violated, and threatening to have the law on you. Might he have a case?

ANSWERS

1. *Under ECHR case law on Article 5, reasonable suspicion can be taken to mean suspicion that would satisfy an objective observer, that a deprivation of liberty was necessary.*

   True, although incomplete. This is not a complete analysis of reasonable suspicion. Having a reasonable suspicion presupposes the existence of facts or information that would satisfy an objective observer that the person concerned might have committed an offence, and not just an honest belief on the part of the person making the arrest that his action is justified.

2. *Strasbourg has not declared an absolute right to silence for the accused in a criminal trial.*

   True. There is a presumption against self-incrimination, but Strasbourg has always sought to ensure that the trial as a whole must be fair, rather than to lay down an inflexible set of rules and procedures for a fair trial. Under some circumstances it may not be a breach of the fairness of the trial as a whole if inferences are drawn from the failure of the accused to answer questions.

3. *The protection of Article 6 applies to civil as well as criminal trials.*
   True.

4. *Strasbourg guarantees the right to trial by jury.*

False. Strasbourg says nothing about the right to trial by jury, which plays no part outside the Anglo-American judicial tradition. However, we might add that since the HRA does not remove the existence of rights that are otherwise recognized, the right to trial by jury remains a fundamental right in the UK.

Some expert commentators have speculated that the right to trial by jury, like the use of non-professional magistrates, will eventually be threatened and perhaps overturned by the impact of HRA. We are not so sure. These institutions may indeed be threatened, for one reason or another. For example, trial by jury was suspended in Northern Ireland because in a climate of terrorism jurors went in fear of their lives. But we do not see the institution of the jury or the lay magistrate as inconsistent with the fundamental principles of human rights. Indeed, we see the lay element of the law as a bastion of liberty and justice, entirely consistent with the protection of human rights in the fullest sense. Here, however, we are wandering outside the boundaries of our question, and must return to the topic in our final chapter.

5. _The ECHR does not apply to servants of the state such as police officers, soldiers or civil servants._

False. The position is more complex. Some rights clearly apply. Other rights may not always apply in full.

6. _Suppose an illegal immigrant has been put on trial for murder, but cannot understand the language of the court. Is he entitled to the free services of an interpreter – even if the case against him is very strong?_

True. He is entitled to the free services of an interpreter, whatever his status or the outcome of the case. Indeed, he is especially in need of this right if the case against him is very strong!

7. _The press may never be excluded from a fair trial._

False. See Article 6 in full. See also Article 10, which will be discussed later.

8. *One of your teachers has been assaulted by an angry parent, whom you have detained by locking him in the storeroom until the police arrive. He is pounding on the locked door, shouting that his rights have been violated, and threatening to have the law on you. Might he have a case?*

He might, although from the sound of it your assaulted teacher has a much better one. Let us remember who is the victim here, and that whatever may have been motivating the parent, that motive cannot justify assault.

You may or may not be a public authority. You may have made a citizen's arrest in this case or simply detained the angry parent by the first means possible. The important point is that your action could be justified on human rights grounds. Much depends upon the circumstances. Let us sketch them in your favour, and suppose that:

– Your intention was to prevent Mr X from causing any further damage to the teacher whom he was assaulting, and the peace of the school that he had disrupted.

– His temporary detention was the necessary and proportionate means to achieve that legitimate objective.

– The police are already responding to your emergency call and will be with you shortly.

– You have asked through the door if Mr X has sustained any injuries. He has simply continued to shout abuse.

Under such circumstances, even the most determined defence lawyer would have to work hard for his client; and his argument would presumably turn upon disputing the facts of the incident rather than its basis in law. Moreover, you are a head teacher and not a trained police officer, anger psychologist or prison warder. Any sensible court would recognize that you may not have been able to calculate to a nicety the degree of force you needed to exert in order to achieve your legitimate objective. The important thing is that the intended outcome was legitimate, and that the actions you took were not disproportionate in themselves – whatever the cause of the original altercation.

7

Respect for private and family life

ARTICLE 8 – THE RIGHT TO RESPECT FOR PRIVATE AND FAMILY LIFE

1. Everyone has the right to respect for his private and family life, his home and his correspondence.

2. There shall be no interference by a public authority with the exercise of this right except such as is in accordance with the law and is necessary in a democratic society in the interests of national security, public safety or the economic well-being of the country, for the prevention of disorder or crime, for the protection of health or morals, or for the protection of the rights and freedoms of others.

For our purposes in this book, Article 8 is probably the most significant article in HRA: for we shall assert that it establishes a new right, and one of widespread potential application.

'I want to be alone' – Greta Garbo

Under common law, it has famously been said that there is no right to privacy. An Englishman's home may be his castle, but this is more rhetoric than reality, and is certainly not a remedy. While there exist some specific potential remedies against some specific breaches of privacy or related offences, there has been no general right or remedy in this area, and we may easily think of examples in which someone's privacy has been invaded and where no obvious redress applied.

PRIVACY, THE PRESS AND THE PUBLIC INTEREST

Consider the person who is being besieged by the press. 'Do you have anything to say, Mr Smith?' asks the broadsheet. 'What have you got, Johnny?' shouts the tabloid. And the unfortunate Mr Smith shuffles away from his doorstep, or wherever the confrontation may be taking place, wishing his affairs had never come to the attention of the media, and falling over an electric cable as he gets into his car.

In such a situation, of course, the media is likely to claim that it is not a public authority and that it has a legitimate public interest in asking for, or indeed demanding, an answer from Mr Smith. It has thus rather cleverly both denied responsibility and claimed a right. In what has been called a post-modern age we are all deeply familiar with such situations, and will probably already have decided what general rules should apply to journalistic behaviour.

For example, we may be of the opinion that politicians should in some broad sense have less expectation of privacy than other people, and should be more robust about such invasions. Their partners, associates and relatives, and especially their children, are entitled to seclusion. They are not. We might extend this notion to people such as athletes, entertainers, or media celebrities themselves, who are normally in or seek the public eye. However, let us concentrate on politicians for the time being.

Politicians should be accountable to the electorate, and are in general past masters at failing to account for their actions. It is indeed in the public interest that they should on occasion be asked questions by the media under circumstances that invade their privacy – for how else is the truth to emerge?

The process needs to be carried out in an acceptable way, with a clear if implicit understanding and acceptance of the rules of the game by both parties, including the possibility of escape. (This norm would seem to work against passive surveillance, such as photography from afar, where the recipient of attention may not even be aware of what is going on – a subject to which we shall return.)

Finally, we may believe that the questions asked should be entirely restricted to matters that are clearly of public interest. Here there is perhaps a greater potential area for ambiguity, and we may need to point out that what the public may be interested in is not necessarily in the public interest.

We might wish to take the classic liberal position, perhaps, that what a minister of state does in his own time is his own affair. But what if that supposedly private conduct reveals a conspicuous absence of judgement, or a sustained capacity for recklessness? Is this the sort of person that we want to be in charge of our defence or foreign policy? (We speak, of course, hypothetically, and without reference to any real politicians, alive or dead.)

What if there is a pattern of sexual or other behaviour that indicates a preference for deviousness and deception, and could leave the minister or other person in authority open to blackmail? What if his behaviour simply shows him to be an immoral person, in the broadest sense, whereas he has stood on a ticket, as the Americans would put it, of morality in public life?

These are challenging issues, and we have widened the debate from privacy to the accountability of politicians in a working democracy. Let us conclude where we started, that there was already a sophisticated public debate in this area before the passage of HRA, and there was a widespread recognition of some need for some general rules on privacy, even if we were not entirely sure as to what they should be. There was a strong view, however, that the private citizen had a right to privacy that the common law did not adequately provide.

Kaye v. Robertson and Another (1991) FSR 62

In this widely publicized case, which was held under domestic law and has led to an appeal to Strasbourg, a well-known actor was lying very seriously injured in a hospital room when two journalists entered and forced an interview. Their actions did not necessarily breach any specific law and it was therefore difficult for the Court of Appeal to grant an injunction forbidding the publication of the interview, although in the end they were able to find grounds to do so. There was no justification for this invasion of privacy on public interest or any other grounds, and it is a good argument for a need for a right to privacy, which may develop in common law. In future, such circumstances as those suffered by Mr Kaye, for example, may allow for action by tort for breach of privacy.

The potential chilling effect of the right to privacy

The fact that some rights clash with each other does not negate the usefulness of ECHR. Such a clash occurs between Articles 8 and 10 – privacy versus freedom of expression. We have already begun to explore the nature of this dilemma in our brief discussion of journalistic practice and in our assumption that many people would support a proportionate invasion of the privacy of politicians by the press in the interest of an accountable democracy, provided that the normal safeguards such as protection against defamation or libel remained in place.

The ECtHR view is that democratic politics is a robust and non-deferential pastime, entered into on a voluntary basis by people who should know and accept the consequences of their choice. A healthy debate means disagreement and criticism, and politicians must expect to be brought to account for the decisions that they make on behalf of the public. For these reasons, the right to freedom of expression is extremely important in public life. However, as we have seen in the Kaye case, that right must not be used to justify completely unacceptable behaviour. The upshot of the argument is that there must be a continuing effort to reconcile these two competing priorities, but not at the expense of the right to privacy having a chilling effect on journalistic freedom of expression.

At the grave risk of over-simplifying the issue, let us say at this stage that we believe in freedom of speech, but not in the right to gather the information that may form the basis for that speech by any means possible. As this is a book about human rights for managers and not the ethics of journalism, we shall leave the debate there, to be returned to in our final chapter.

WHERE THE RIGHT TO PRIVACY APPLIES

Article 8 states that everyone has the right to respect for his private and family life, his home and his correspondence. There is a notion here of a private space: an area in which people are free to be themselves, without let or hindrance. But the right simply to be left alone may not fully satisfy our need to express ourselves as human beings. There is a positive right here, as well as a negative freedom.

To consider the proper extent of privacy is to ponder what it means to be human, and where the state can do most good – or harm. Bear with us as we reveal our own predilections and preferences in this area. In our view writers should acknowledge and work with their views, for to attempt to hide or deny them is in reality to indicate their existence all the more strongly; and we shall not try.

There is a changing concept of freedom, so that what is acceptable in one era is not acceptable in another, and vice versa. It is facile to assume that the freedom to live as one chooses is continually expanding along some linear notion of progress towards a point of perfect freedom. History tells us that as one restriction is removed, another may be imposed. Our children, for example, may not be subjected to the same discipline as their parents or grandparents, at school or in the home. They may have a different means of access to information, through modern technology. But if they cannot walk or bicycle from home to school and back in freedom, then they do not have the same freedom as earlier generations, nor the same opportunity to grow and develop by direct observation of life, rather than by mediated contact.

Contrast the reality of meeting a cow, for example, with the synthetic pleasure of being introduced to her by a breathless commentator on a television programme – an encounter, moreover, which does not allow for the extraordinary sensation of milking!

Changing means of communication

Correspondence has been taken to include, over the years, means of communication that did not exist in 1950, or did not exist for most people. Thus, for example, we may claim the right to privacy in regard to our e-mail or mobile telephones. As the means by which we can communicate expand, so may the problems that the new technology brings with it. For example, there are the vexed questions of who is to police the Internet, or the proper responsibilities of Internet Service Providers, as addressed in the Government's new Regulation in Procedures Act, 2000. Whatever the technological changes we face, the right to privacy will need to be reconciled with them by means of legislation in parliament and challenge in court.

The expectation of privacy

The right to privacy is claimed more readily where we have a legitimate expectation of privacy. We may have an extremely strong expectation of privacy within the four walls where we eat, sleep and read books on human rights. We have some expectation of respect for our privacy, however, in the garden, or in the garden shed, or even on our way to the local public house in conversation with friends. In that situation there may be a collective assumption of privacy, so that if a newcomer wishes to join in or disrupt the conversation he must be invited – although a mobile telephone caller will probably be exempted from this rule!

Rights must be taken seriously

ECHR was framed in the aftermath of totalitarian behaviour, and is primarily intended to prevent its repetition. Both Nazis and Communists set out to attack and weaken or destroy the essence of family life and its associated privacy as a threat to the overwhelming power of the state, and the rightfulness of its prevailing ideology. Children, for example, were encouraged to denounce their parents for such offences as bourgeois revisionism; and all citizens were encouraged to inform against their neighbours for their political opinions or racial origins. Those are fundamental violations of universal norms, and it is they, rather than questions to do with the etiquette of the use of the mobile telephone, which ECHR exists to address.

We may note that revolutions and stable family life do not usually go together, and recognize that ECHR is, to some extent, a song of triumph to the bourgeois concept of freedom. We must also acknowledge that the benefits of that freedom extend beyond the right to wash our car on a Saturday morning on our own driveway, before loading it up with undesirable items for the church fête. The benefits of bourgeois freedom extend to any lifestyle that does not harm others, and benefit conformist and non-conformist alike.

WHAT IS A FAMILY?

Family life need not be confined to the notion of a family as in the advertiser's dream – mother, father, and two relaxed and smiling children, all prepared to buy the latest product in order to complete their domestic bliss in leafy suburbia. A family need not be rich, successful or respectable, and it need not be permanently united. Indeed, the parameters of what is a family are constantly being tested, and Strasbourg has had to be particularly careful in keeping pace with social norms in this area. On the whole, it has been cautious in interpreting ECHR in such a way as to develop and expand the rights of would-be immigrants, or long-sentence prisoners, or in other areas of strong political controversy.

Nevertheless, there has been a judicial willingness to question the basis on which some decisions in member states have been made. There are a number of cases dealing with issues such as the right to have a change of sex recognized by the state, which may not directly affect the lives and happiness of large numbers of people, but which are extremely important to those who are affected by them, and where Strasbourg has provided a service unobtainable elsewhere by being prepared to probe the reasoning of the relevant state in its decision making and to bring it to account for its actions.

A PRIVATE LIFE AT WORK

Respect for private life must also comprise to a certain degree the right to establish and develop relationships with other human beings. There appears, furthermore, to be no reason of principle why this understanding of the notion of 'private life' should be taken to exclude activities of a professional or business nature since it is, after all, in the course of their working lives that the majority of people have a significant, if not the greatest, opportunity of developing relationships with the outside world. (Niemitz v. Germany (1992) 16 EHRR 97)

We have a legitimate expectation of privacy at work for many reasons. We spend much of our time at work. It is an important part of our lives as a whole, and not just a source of income. Our employer has no overall justification to invade or restrict that privacy, but must find a specific reason for a specific violation. Work is not slavery, but a freely accepted contractual obligation, and we do not give up our rights by going to work (or by working at home).

On the other hand, the manager may feel that here is a very slippery slope. If the employee claims a right to privacy at work, what are the limitations to that right, and what further alleged right might next be claimed? In rhetorical terms, the right to manage is being threatened, and that cannot be tolerated.

There is, of course, no specific right to manage under the ECHR. Nevertheless, it is an evocative phrase. Any manager has an obligation to carry out his task or tasks to the best of his abilities, for only thus can he properly fulfil his responsibilities. As a professional manager he needs some discretion or freedom to manoeuvre: but _not_ the freedom to violate employees', shareholders' or customers' rights.

The employee may have some expectation of privacy at work. However, in going to work at all he has accepted that there will be some constraints upon both his privacy and his freedom. What is important is that those constraints are both known and lawful, that their exercise is both necessary and proportionate, and that the process satisfies the canon of accountability in the widest sense. How all this could work out in practice can be best evaluated in case studies, to which we now turn.

CASE STUDIES

Surveillance at work

There is a problem with internal theft in a retail company, and the solution chosen by senior management has been to mount concealed cameras in strategic places so that employees who are stealing from the till or in some other way cheating the system, can be detected and dealt with. What are the human rights issues here?

Commentary

Firstly, the company would need to consider its status as a private organization or public authority, and its legal position. If it is a public authority, for example, its activities are governed by the Regulation in Procedures Act, 2000.

Secondly, there is a general issue of the invasion of privacy here. The company should make sure:

▓ that there is a serious problem to address in the first place;

▓ that it has exhausted the possibilities of less intrusive means before it considers this measure;

▓ that the measure once attempted is reasonably likely to lead to the desired outcome (ie it produces valid and usable evidence);

▓ that the measure is applied to suspected parties, as far as possible, and not to those whom there is no reason to suspect of wrong doing; and

▓ that measures exist to deal with collateral damage (eg, private information that may be discovered but that was not being looked for and is not relevant to the original purpose of the inquiry).

Thirdly, we would suggest that the company in question reads and considers any general guidance that may have been produced by the government, the legal profession, or any relevant professional organization, on the rights and wrongs of the use of surveillance on private territory. There may be a code that applies.

Fourthly, we would suggest that the company might consider the alternative possibility of mounting unconcealed surveillance cameras, as a general precaution against theft.

Private investigations

A newly created specialist agency for the investigation and reduction of benefit fraud has begun to use the services of private detectives in investigating cases where it is believed that employees, with or without the knowledge and support of their employers, are fraudulently claiming benefit while also working. The main company that the agency has started to employ, faircop.com, is composed almost entirely of ex-police officers and customs officials, and appears to be highly efficient. Their favoured methods appear to be threefold:

1. to mount surveillance operations;

2. to put people into suspected organizations and report on what is going on; and

3. to obtain access to confidential information through previously established official contacts and use it for commercial purposes.

What are the human rights issues?

Commentary

There could be a number of human rights issues arising in such circumstances, in regard to the invasion of privacy, the right to a fair trial, possible discrimination and other issues. We shall briefly discuss some of the issues that might arise.

The status of faircop.com. The agency may be a public authority. It might be argued that any organization which is working for them, such as faircop.com, is also a public authority while working *pro bono publico* and carrying out a task which the parent organization would have to find a way of doing for itself if faircop.com's services were not available. Faircop.com must therefore respect and uphold human rights, and is not an extra-legal alternative.

Surveillance operations. These may be or amount to an unjustified invasion of privacy, and there is some case law in this area. The greater the expectation of privacy, the greater the invasion. Following, photographing or using CCTV to observe someone in the street (in order to establish, perhaps, his whereabouts or company at a certain time) is hardly a serious invasion of privacy. Putting a secret camera in his bedroom is clearly:

▨ illegal;

▨ a gross invasion of privacy; and

▨ an entirely unnecessary means of attempting to establish whether or not he is fraudulently claiming unemployment benefit.

In between these two extremes is an infinite range of actions, where the possible invasion of privacy must be assessed by comparing fact with principle.

The use of undercover agents. While this is a favourite (and morally neutral) topic of fiction, we sometimes wonder just how much of it is actually going on, and to what extent it may be necessary. There is clearly an element of deception in the use of an undercover agent, but deception is not necessarily an invasion of privacy, and nor need it raise profound issues. Agents, sleepers and spies who lead a double life for a prolonged period may betray friendships, family life and finally themselves, but casual, limited and short-term deception is, we would suggest, an everyday part of life. Consider, for example, the manager who telephones his organization in order to assess the quality of its response, but without revealing his true identity. Do we censure his cunning, or acknowledge the virtue of a limited ploy?

We would suggest that in the case of investigating fraudulent unemployment benefit claims, it might be both necessary and proportionate to make use of undisclosed investigators, provided that they eschew obvious illegalities such as acting as *agents provocateurs*, and thereby creating crimes that would not otherwise have occurred (the same principle is useful in so-called 'sting' operations). Passive investigation of what would have occurred in any case is one thing: causing it to happen is another. The manager is responsible for the health and safety of his clandestine employees, and should take reasonable precautions to protect them from any adverse consequences of their deception. There may be issues about the quality and objectivity of the evidence if the matter goes to trial.

Misuse of confidential information. Although this could be portrayed as a trivial offence against bureaucratic regulations, it is in fact, we believe, the basis for a serious breach of human rights.

If a former police officer is able, for example, to obtain access to confidential information such as criminal records or intelligence records by exploiting his old contacts, then one unlawful act may constitute a series of offences and have widespread consequences. Breach of confidentiality can have very serious consequences, and not just in the area of medical records.

This is an important area, and one to which we shall return in depth in our final chapter, when we consider the right to be informed. In the meantime, let us emphasize that the misuse or abuse of confidential information is likely to be a breach not only of human rights but also of the Data Protection Act and other legislation.

Cold calling

Company operatives make unsolicited ('cold') telephone calls to potential customers as a regular part of its marketing strategy. Some recipients object, and claim that such a strategy amounts to an invasion of their human rights. Is it?

Commentary

We assume this issue will certainly be tested in court. In the meantime, here are some general comments. Unsolicited telephone calls could well be seen as an invasion of privacy, and a nuisance to boot. They could be claimed to interrupt the recipient's peaceful enjoyment of his possessions. He might claim that the manner in which he had been chosen to receive the call in the first place was an example of discrimination.

However, this is an area where the citizen may not be able to claim a complete expectation of privacy in the first place. If someone buys a telephone and lists his number in a telephone directory, he may reasonably expect that unknown people may call him, just as he may receive unsolicited mail through the post.

Secondly, the instrument of proportionality applies. The manner and persistence of the cold caller may turn a welcome call or minor irritation into a serious nuisance. If the caller becomes a real nuisance then there are legal remedies available; but that does not mean that there is no intermediate breach of human rights.

Finally, while it is not clear that it is in the public interest that salesmen should be able to make unsolicited calls, nor is the reverse obviously true. There could be an actionable invasion of privacy occurring in such a situation. However, it should be possible to prevent such an outcome by careful selection and training of the appropriate employees by the company that has chosen to follow this policy. There is a very good case for invading employees' privacy by monitoring the content and style of the calls they make, in order to make sure that no offence is being caused!

Congress

Mrs Evans is the office manager of a small branch of a large commercial enterprise. Two of its employees, Miss Arnold and Mr Braithwaite, are having an affair, which has come to her attention through office gossip. Miss Arnold is single but cohabiting with Mr Cash, who works for a rival company. Mr Braithwaite is married. His wife Denise, who is partially disabled, does not go out to work.

Mrs Evans does not know how long this affair has been going on, and has no official proof of its existence. Nevertheless, the gossip both from her own office and other branches of the same company, together with circumstantial evidence and her own intuition, leads her to be sure of its reality.

The company norm is to disapprove of such affairs and the approved action is that the manager should separate those involved.

Mrs Evans decides to move Miss Arnold to another office in another branch of the same company, within the same city. Miss Arnold is junior to Mr Braithwaite, and her circumstances are such that a move will cause her less disruption.

Miss Arnold objects to being told to move, and insists on knowing the reason, which Mrs Evans had not revealed. Mrs Evans tells her that it is because of the affair, which is against company policy. However, Mrs Evans had no intention of broadcasting this reason to all employees. As far as she was concerned, the matter is confidential. There are many other reasons why Miss Arnold may move, and Mrs Evans does not intend to publish the true one.

Miss Arnold objects to her manager's decision as a breach of her human rights. Is it?

Commentary

There may be some possible breaches of a number of rights here, including 6, 8 and 14. Let us work our way through some of the issues, raising points of wider application.

If we can establish that company policy both exists and is widely known, then neither party can claim that the consequences of their action in having an office affair were unknown to them.

We are, however, still at liberty to ask if the company needs a policy in such an area. Is it the proper business of the company to investigate and control the sexual behaviour of its employees? This is not a legal question, and cannot be answered by such means, but it does need to be addressed.

Both Miss Arnold and Mr Braithwaite have a right to a private life, and that private life includes some aspects of their working lives (see *Niemitz v. Germany*, 1992, quoted earlier in this chapter). However, the right to a private life is not unconditional, and the activity in question is hardly of a professional nature. Article 8 allows for the invasion of privacy 'for the protection of health or morals', but that is a matter for the state to regulate and not a private company. Moreover, we would suppose that in this case the company is seeking to preserve effective working relationships, rather than the sanctity of marriage *per se*.

Is Miss Arnold entitled to the protection of Article 6 in this case, and if so, has it been breached? The company could assert that this is an administrative matter, and that Article 6 does not apply. A human rights counter-argument is that it does, since this situation could lead to a dismissal. The question then becomes, are company procedures in this area reconcilable with the fundamental precepts of a fair trial?

That will depend upon an examination of the procedures in question, and goes beyond hypothesis to reality. However, the scenario reads to suggest that the manager in question has considerable discretionary powers and does not appear to need to account for her actions. These are danger signals, for they may lead to arbitrary or unfair actions. We do not know whether or not Miss Arnold has an internal right of appeal, but it is a relevant issue. The element of confidentiality in this situation, and the possibility of bargaining between manager and employee, both complicate the matter.

Article 14 is limited to discrimination in connection with the violation of other rights. In this case, other rights could be taken to apply, and Miss Arnold seems to have been chosen as the sacrificial lamb. Why should she be moved, or face dismissal, rather than Mr Braithwaite? Has Mrs Evans discriminated against her, and could that discrimination possibly be justified? If we are seeking to find the least intrusive method by which this situation could be rectified, we could argue that only one party should be moved, and that party should be chosen on grounds of least disruption. However, there may be other values being applied here, which will no doubt be the subject of discussion!

Sex change

One of a small and non-unionized company's employees proclaims that she has changed her sex from male to female, and claims the right to be treated as a woman at work and to be known henceforth as Jenny rather than Jim Owens. Other employees refuse to acknowledge and accept her change of sex, ridicule her at every opportunity, and object to her sharing the lavatories provided for either male or female employees.

The manager, Mr Burroughs, states that Jenny's behaviour has made her unemployable and is affecting production, and that he has no alternative but to fire her.

What are the human rights issues in this situation, and how might it have been otherwise resolved?

Commentary

In accord with the spirit of human rights, Jenny, like any other human being, deserves to be treated with respect. Moreover, the ECtHR has constantly asserted that a democratic society should practise the virtues of pluralism, broad-mindedness and tolerance towards differing lifestyles, and those virtues are not being demonstrated in this case.

The ridicule to which Jenny is being subjected at work violates the principle of respect. In more specific terms, it may be construed as constituting humiliating and degrading treatment in violation of Article 3. Jenny has an absolute right not be humiliated and degraded to the extent that it is considered to violate that Article, and there are no conditions or circumstances that can be held to justify such behaviour. It is therefore irrelevant to any argument based upon Article 3, that she could be argued to have brought that ridicule upon herself. Nor can the manager claim that it would be a disproportionate exertion on his part to change his policies and procedures because one person chooses to behave differently. That is the whole point of having a right.

Jenny has the right, or in this case more appropriately the fundamental freedom, not to be humiliated, and she cannot alienate that right by her own behaviour. In addition, she has the right to a private life, and she has the right not to be discriminated against on unlawful grounds in her enjoyment of her other rights. She may not have the right under national law to change her sex, but she does have the right to be recognized and treated as whom she claims to be. She does not have the right to work, as such, but she does not need to claim such a right in this case in order to address the problems that she is facing.

Finally, may we make some general points. Firstly, there is nothing in ECHR that prohibits a manager from working to reach a solution to a problem, and we would suggest that there is a range of possible courses of non-legal action open to the manager in this case, which could fruitfully be discussed amongst a group of readers of this book. Secondly, we do not need a Human Rights Act to identify that this is a highly undesirable state of affairs that should have been prevented from developing. Although we do not know the pattern of events preceding her declaration, we wonder that Jim could not have become Jenny with rather less disastrous consequences at work, whether by more careful management or a more enlightened attitude on the part of the workforce, or a combination of the two. The blunt instrument of the law is a last resort, and prevention is usually better than cure.

Investigation

You run a small high technology company employing highly skilled and self-motivated professionals who spend much of their working time absorbed electronically. Your style of management is very much to delegate, monitor progress, and occasionally reassure, advise or coach. You may have to formally correct someone's behaviour, but this is rare. First, they are likely to be far more expert in what they are doing than you, and must be given some discretion. Secondly, if their work is consistently going wrong it is more sensible to fire and replace them than to attempt to correct the fault. In the volatile and fast-changing environment in which you manage, that is regarded as normal and acceptable behaviour, and contracts are drawn up accordingly.

This is not the sort of business in which is it is either appropriate or even possible for you to know exactly what everyone is doing all the time, or with whom they may need to be in contact. Like journalists, they have their sources – and you tend to judge their work by its results.

As a result of a random check, your security expert finds evidence that appears to indicate that one of your employees, Sylvia Jenkins, has been regularly carrying out private business in company time and on company equipment. You decide to investigate further. Your security expert tells you that if he is to do his job properly, he will need to investigate all of Ms Jenkins' e-mails, since she was in the habit of mixing work, private business and pleasure, and they are inextricably combined. It is also apparent that Ms Jenkins mixed work and pleasure throughout her life, so that she sent private messages from work and business messages from home.

He carries out some further investigations, as a result of which you decide that Ms Jenkins must be dismissed forthwith. Company regulations can be read in such a way as to justify this, and you cannot imagine how she could justify her actions. But you are a cautious person, and before you proceed to action, you pause to think for a moment about human rights. What are the human rights issues here, and is there any way in which Ms Jenkins could use the new HRA to her advantage?

Commentary

Although there would no doubt be complications in real life, we see the essence of this scenario as relatively simple, from the human rights perspective.

There is a possible issue of the right to privacy, and the necessity and proportionality of the actions of the employer in invading the privacy of Ms Jenkins' correspondence. (He might have known enough to act, already. He might have looked for evidence elsewhere. He might have asked Ms Jenkins what she was doing.)

No doubt Ms Jenkins could argue that as she has certainly been carrying out official business in her own time, she should be given some latitude in carrying out her own business in the firm's time. That, however, is not the whole of what is at issue. On the face of it, Ms Jenkins' approach has been deceitful; she may have been guilty of financial irregularity, if not double-dealing; and her activities once revealed are likely to bring the firm into disrepute. She has no right to privacy in order to defraud her employer, and provided its policies are clear, known and followed it should, in our opinion, have a strong case.

8

Freedom of thought, conscience and religion

ARTICLE 9 – FREEDOM OF THOUGHT, CONSCIENCE AND RELIGION

1. Everyone has the right to freedom of thought, conscience and religion; this right includes freedom to change his religion or belief and freedom, either alone or in community with others and in public or private, to manifest his religion or belief, in worship, teaching, practice and observance.

2. There shall be no interference by a public authority with the exercise of this right except such as is in accordance with the law and is necessary in a democratic society in the interests of national security, public safety or the economic well-being of the country, for the prevention of disorder or crime, for the protection of health or morals, or for the protection of the rights and freedoms of others.

Part one of this article recognizes the absolute right to freedom of thought, conscience and religion. Part two qualifies the manifestation of that religion or those beliefs, for set reasons.

In a modern, secular, pluralist society it might be thought that either this right is no longer needed – like a right to breathe, it may be taken for granted – or that it requires no special protection and is unlikely to generate any real controversy. Both assumptions would be wrong. In 1998 parliament believed religious freedom to be of particular importance, and the HRA was modified accordingly in Section 13:

> *Freedom of thought, conscience and religion*
> *13 (1) If a court's determination of any question arising under this Act might affect the exercise by a religious organization (itself or its members collectively) of the Convention right to freedom of thought, conscience and religion, it must have particular regard to the importance of that right.*
> *13 (2) In this section 'court' includes a tribunal.*

Secondly, although there have been few challenges at Strasbourg which have arisen as a result of a breach of this right, it has given rise to some controversial decisions. Finally, the right to religious observance may well cause problems for the manager at work, or in any closed institution. Rather than continue in the abstract, let us immediately consider a hypothetical case, to which we shall attach the relevant case law. If you are able to address this case with other people and to sample the variation of opinion that may be expected to occur, so much the better.

The case of Janet Isaacson

Janet Isaacson works for a large organization, which puts considerable pressure upon its managers but at the same time rewards them handsomely. Her contract states not the number of hours that she is required to work but that she should complete her tasks to the appropriate standard, and so far this has caused her no serious difficulties. The company norm is that people work hard and play hard. If there is work to be done, people do it, and will often work late into the evening or come in at weekends. At the same time, the managing director is generous in funding corporate hospitality and pays good bonuses when profits are up, so that she was at first happy with her conditions of employment.

Over the past few months, however, Janet has become rather unhappy. There is a new managing director with a very different personality to her predecessor, and she appears to demand as a right what he requested as a privilege. Matters have come to a head over working on Sundays.

Sundays are special to Janet, a practising Christian, and while she does not go so far as to think that one should never work on a Sunday, she believes that it should be generally a day of rest, recuperation and quiet worship. However, her colleagues, most of whom joined the company straight from university and are still in their twenties, have got into the habit of meeting on Sunday mornings in order to prepare for the next week. The formal gathering is followed by a good lunch at the company's expense, to which spouses, partners and children are always invited. The new Managing Director has been known to refer to her team as one big happy family, and she appears, at least in Janet's opinion, to live to work rather than to work to live.

Janet objects to what is happening on two grounds. First, there is an element of compulsion about the whole process, all the more effective through not being expressed in terms of outright coercion. Anyone who voices disquiet at this forced socialization is portrayed as not being a good sport, or otherwise marginalized. When Janet did say something the new boss simply replied: 'Welcome to the 21st century, Janet.'

Janet feels that the regular Sunday gathering is both unnecessary and a gross invasion of privacy to boot: what has happened to her right to a family life? When can one pursue that, if not at the weekend? And why should the fact that she does not actually have an immediate family to care for make any difference to that right?

Secondly, she feels that the Sunday morning gathering inter-feres with her right to freedom of worship, since she can no longer attend Matins at her local church. She raises these points in informal conversation with another manager who has a degree in law. He passes over the first point and answers the second by suggesting alternative forms of worship that are still open to her. For example, why should Janet not go to Communion or Evensong, and still be free to demonstrate commitment and solidarity during the middle of the day? Is it really so very onerous to have a drink with her colleagues and enjoy a splendid lunch at the company's expense? After all, she is not a religious fanatic, is she? She has already conceded that she would not object to meeting on a Sunday if there were a clear and inescapable need. In reality it is the only time when very busy people can actually get together and share each other's company in a relaxed and informal atmosphere. The others don't object; and clearly, if someone is going away for the weekend, then their presence is not required. Isn't she in danger of creating a storm in a teacup, when she really thinks about it?

Commentary

There is something very iffy about this whole arrangement, at least in my pre-21st-century view, and I would object very strongly to being treated in such a way. On the other hand, I might not last very long in a contemporary high pressure/high rewards working environment! There are three questions that we need to ask:

1. Are these Sunday meetings really necessary? We suspect that the answer to that must be, no. We can imagine circumstances, given the nature of modern communications, when some people will have to work at weekends, or even during major festivities such as Christmas. In fact, this has always been required of certain occupations. But there is a difference between genuine and presumed necessity, especially when there is no real scrutiny of the basis for the action, and that leads to our second question.

2. Are these meetings voluntary or compulsory? There is a strong argument for saying that they are compulsory, even if not backed by law or regulation. We may be compelled by norms as well as by law, and moral coercion, as John Stuart Mill recognized, can be very effective. While there is evidence of a formal freedom to dissent here, we may infer that there are strong pressures to conform. If the meetings are a compulsory part of working life then that should be made clear, and debate take place as to how such compulsory attendance will affect those who joined the job under different conditions and expectations.

3. Is this a human rights issue? We believe that the answer here must be yes, even if there may be other ways of resolving the problem than in court. The right to respect for private and family life means a life of the individual's own choosing, and not a substitute welfare scheme dreamt up by the employer. We may argue our case here on a strict interpretation of Article 8. We may also refer to the spirit of human rights, and the background, which led to the creation of ECHR in the first place. Totalitarian societies set out to extinguish the informality and indiscipline of normal family life and replace it by the enterprise of the state, whether by the Hitler Youth or the Young Communists. Freedom of choice includes the option to make a perverse or self-damaging choice, unless it can be shown that there are valid human rights reasons against it. It is for the individual to make the choice of lifestyle, whether that be to embrace Christianity, Rastafarianism, Scientology, or any other belief, including no belief at all; and not the employer on her behalf.

Secondly, we must consider Janet's claim to the right to manifest her religion. Clearly, she has that right. Clearly, it was not as a rule interfered with when she first began working for her current employers. And it is at least strongly arguable that there is now some infringement of that right. Does her legally trained colleague David have a case? An advocate could certainly make one. The right to privacy is qualified and not absolute, and the right to manifest one's religion must take the circumstances into account: as Janet herself acknowledged in recognizing that certain occupations require one to work on holy days. But if we consider the two rights, 8 and 9, in combination, it is a strong one.

What does Strasbourg case law tell us here? Strasbourg judges would appear to recognize the reality of commercial life, and are certainly not biased in favour of the Christian religion, or any other. As we have said before, it is their duty to attempt to apply broad principles to the varied panoply of life in Europe, with its differing traditions, mores and values, and we shall not look to them for absolute judgement in this area. There is one case which appears especially apposite, and which we shall now discuss.

Stedman v. United Kingdom, 23 EHRR CD 169

The applicant, a practising Christian, was dismissed by a private company as a result of refusing to sign a contract that would have obliged her to work some Sundays on a rota basis. She argued unfair dismissal in that her rights 6, 8, 9 and 14 had been breached.

Let us first of all note in passing that this case reached the ECtHR even though Ms Stedman's employer was not a public authority, and then go on to consider the issues involved in some depth.

The Commission found no breach of human rights, and dismissed the appeal. Why? They judged that she was still free to hold and practise her religion, if necessary by resigning from the company in question. That company was not forcing her to change or abandon her religion: they were simply laying down certain terms and conditions under which she would be expected to work. In the modern world those conditions were not necessarily unreasonable, and there was no evidence that Ms Stedman was being discriminated against in their application.

Comment

We find this judgement surprising. We accept that ECHR does not guarantee the right to work *per se*, that work does impose certain constraints upon one's lifestyle, and that the right to a private life is not an unqualified one. We understand that while a person is free to hold a certain religion, he does not have an unfettered right to practise it. But we remain puzzled, and wonder what would have been the reaction if Ms Stedman had been free to raise the relevant human rights issues in an English court, rather than being obliged to wend the long and expensive path to Strasbourg. Would an English judge have been quite so fastidious in his unwillingness to find an unjustified violation of human rights? We do not know: but we think that he might have found more favour in the applicant's case than was found in Strasbourg.

In sum, we do not find this case truly analogous to the hypothetical one that we have previously offered. Our conclusion is that any company should think long and hard before it imposes any policy which could be seen as attacking the opportunity for the traditional practice of family life or religious worship, and especially hard before it does anything that could be seen as an attack on both.

The employee has the right to know the terms and conditions under which he will be expected to work before he takes on the job, and that those terms and conditions will not be changed unfairly or arbitrarily. Both parties are under an obligation to respect the initial agreement, and if it is to be changed that process must be negotiated.

CASE STUDIES

A religious challenge

Mr Fadl'Allah, who has worked for you for 10 years, announces that he has become a Muslim and no longer intends to work on Fridays. It is his right to do this under the ECHR, and any action on your part will be a breach of those rights. What is your response?

Commentary

Mr Fadl'Allah has the right to become a Muslim. He is guaranteed that right under ECHR Article 9.1, which states that the right to freedom of thought, conscience and religion includes the freedom to change one's religion. The right is absolute.

However, there is a subtle difference between declaring or adopting a religion and practising it, as we have already seen in the case of Ms Stedman. The former is an absolute right, but the latter is qualified.

In this case, Mr Fadl'Allah knew that he would have to work on Fridays when he joined the organization, and therefore cannot claim that he has been treated unfairly or arbitrarily in being expected to continue to do so. The company has not prevented him from becoming a Muslim, since he is at liberty to leave that job and seek a position elsewhere. (As we have seen earlier, ECHR does not guarantee a right to work.) Provided that the terms and conditions of employment are legal, clear and reasonable and do not discriminate unfairly against particular employees, Mr Fadl'Allah would seem to lack a case in human rights.

The sensible organization, of course, would not necessarily set out to resolve this issue purely on the grounds of a formal interpretation of the human rights issues involved, although it is a useful bottom line. Is there some way in which the interests of Mr Fadl'Allah and the organization can be reconciled, so that each party achieves what it wants? That is a matter for analysis and negotiation in the particular circumstances of the case in point, and does not lend itself to a general judgement. It may be, however, the better managerial solution.

Quaking and shaking

The company in question, Quakertoys, was begun and developed by people of strong religious faith and has always attempted to do business according to the highest moral standards. It has treated its workforce better than the law required, and over the years has generally provided a happy and supportive working and living environment for its employees. Labour relations have been good and the workforce has never been unionized. People tend to work for the company for life, and many employees are the sons and daughters, or even the grandchildren or great-grandchildren, of former employees.

Over the years there has been an unwritten tradition that the company looked favourably on the recruitment and promotion of people of strong moral and religious conviction, and the majority of company employees are practising Christians.

Dispute has recently arisen over a company policy that was once accepted without question. Matters have been brought to a head by the case of Georgina Chopes, an unmarried mother of two children who has been working for the company for the past seven years and has been twice ignored for promotion, despite her impressive qualifications and excellent work record. Ms Chopes has not raised any issue herself, but others are concerned on her behalf, and are claiming that she is being discriminated against because she is unmarried, is politically active in radical causes, and is not a practising Christian.

What are the human rights issues here?

Commentary

Any company is entitled to celebrate and maintain its traditions, but not to break the law in their furtherance. There appears to be a real issue of unfair discrimination here, although it could be difficult to prove in court. ECHR exists for the benefit of victims and not the political ambitions of their supporters, and it is for Ms Chopes to claim the status of victim and not others on her behalf. There are other means in law of addressing this grievance, which may be more suitable in this case.

Back to school

A school founded and still supported and maintained by a religious charity has advertised for a new teacher and stated that the position is only open to those who follow and practise the faith in question. The school educates its pupils within the context of that faith, and its teachers will be part of an organized religious community and have pastoral as well as teaching responsibilities.

Is this policy illegitimate under the Human Rights Act?

Commentary

Let us be bold, and say no, we think not. Although the issue would need to be tested in a court, this sounds like legitimate discrimination, and is why the HRA includes Paragraph 13.

9

Freedom of expression, assembly and association

ARTICLE 10 – FREEDOM OF EXPRESSION

1. Everyone has the right to freedom of expression. This right shall include freedom to hold opinions and to receive and impart information and ideas without interference by public authority and regardless of frontiers. This Article shall not prevent States from requiring the licensing of broadcasting, television or cinema enterprises.

2. The exercise of these freedoms, since it carries with it duties and responsibilities, may be subject to such formalities, conditions, restrictions or penalties as are prescribed by law and are necessary in a democratic society, in the interests of national security, territorial integrity or public safety, for the prevention of disorder of crime, for the protection of health or morals, for the protection of the reputation or rights of others,

for preventing the disclosure of information received in confidence, or for maintaining the authority and impartiality of the judiciary.

ARTICLE 11 – FREEDOM OF ASSEMBLY AND ASSOCIATION

1. Everyone has the right to freedom of peaceful assembly and to freedom of association with others, including the right to form and to join trade unions for the protection of his interests.

2. No restrictions shall be placed on the exercise of these rights other than such as are prescribed by law and are necessary in a democratic society in the interests of national security or public safety, for the prevention of disorder or crime, for the protection of health or morals or for the protection of the rights and freedoms of others. This Article shall not prevent the imposition of lawful restrictions on the exercise of these rights by members of the armed forces, of the police or of the administration of the State.

HUMAN RIGHTS ACT, 1998

Freedom of expression

12 (4) The court must have particular regard to the importance of the Convention right to freedom of expression and, where the proceedings relate to material which the respondent claims, or which appears to the court, to be journalistic, literary or artistic material (or to conduct connected with such material), to –
(a) the extent to which –
(i) the material has, or is about to, become available to the public; or
(ii) it is, or would be, in the public interest for the material to be published:
(b) any relevant privacy code.

Articles 9, 10 and 11 are linked. We have the right first, to think freely; secondly, to express those thoughts freely; and thirdly, to join together with others in expressing those thoughts. All three rights offer more than this, and all are qualified. There is a logical sequence to their ordering, and in many cases they will all apply. In such cases, Strasbourg has sometimes chosen to investigate the breach of one article only. A domestic court may choose to investigate breaches of all three, for example if this will affect the penalty awarded.

Commentary on Article 10

We explored Article 9 in the previous chapter. Having formed our thoughts, we must be able to express them. Freedom of expression is the cornerstone of a liberal democracy and the essence of John Stuart Mill's seminal essay on liberty to which we referred in Chapter 1.

ECHR recognizes that the right to freedom of expression is of limited advantage to those who have been deprived of access to the relevant information on which to form a considered opinion, and hence states that the right includes 'freedom to receive and impart information and ideas without interference by public authority and regardless of frontiers'. Is this the equivalent of a full right to freedom of information? By no means. But it is a useful start and we will return to this topic in our final chapter.

Article 10 is heavily qualified, and there are a large number of possible reasons under which a public authority may be justified in interfering with the right to freedom of expression. However, we must note that the list of possible grounds for interference, although lengthy, is both finite and exhaustive; and in any case of appeal, judges may be expected to scrutinize very carefully the reasons given for any interference with this right, with the principle of proportionality well to the fore.

There is a particular danger with the right to freedom of expression, in that too zealous an interference by the state may attack the 'very essence' of the right in question. Having said that, we must also recognize that on occasion public authorities may have not only the option but also the obligation to restrict, censor and ban free expression, in order, for example, to protect the rights of others. For the artist, censorship may be a dirty word; but censorship does not only apply to artistic expression. There is no freedom to shout: 'Fire!' in a crowded cinema, and there are many other equally justified restrictions upon freedom of expression that do not touch upon artistic freedom.

Finally, we note that parliament paid special attention to the right to freedom of expression, as is shown in the above quotation from Section 12 of the Act, which links together journalistic, literary and artistic material in relation to the right in question.

Commentary on Article 11

Protest

Article 11 puts together the right to peaceful protest and the right to join a trade union or association and take part in its activities (although ECHR does not support the closed shop, and cannot be read as promoting an absolute right to strike or take other industrial action).

In a functioning democracy the right to peaceful protest is seen as immensely important, and a public authority such as the police, which is responsible for maintaining public order, must not only acknowledge this right but take active measures to protect its exercise. Thus if, for example, a demonstration is planned by Group X which is likely to lead to a counter-demonstration by Group Y, the police cannot simply ban the demonstration in the interests of keeping the peace, even if the counter-demonstration is likely to attract extremists and to be violent.

Proportionality dictates that the police may only restrict a legitimate right to the extent that it is necessary to achieve a legitimate aim, and there may be other ways of preventing the undesirable consequences of a violent counter-demonstration by Group Y than by banning the original demonstration. (Moreover, if Group X's demonstration were banned, it would be as if they were being punished for others' misdemeanours, which would be an unsatisfactory state of affairs.)

The ECtHR recognizes that the resources of a public authority such as the police are limited. Nevertheless, it will not accept this as a blanket excuse for failing to protect human rights such as the right to freedom of expression, or any other right. The Court is concerned with what we might call the 'quality of management' exercised by the police as a public authority: in other words, the intelligence and foresight with which it anticipates, plans and trains for operations so that it is *not* caught out, even by the tactically unexpected.

Thus it is not a sufficient answer for the police, or any other public authority facing an analogous problem, to say that it could not safeguard a demonstration because it had faced an unexpected demand or demands. A little more evidence than that would be needed as to the measures in operation in that force to cope both with the expected and the unexpected, before the court could be satisfied that this was a reasonable explanation and not an easy excuse.

The decision as to what to do about a demonstration at a particular time and place will usually rest with the police (or with the Independent Parades Commission in Northern Ireland). Other than in the case of judicial review, a court reviews the basis for a decision after the event.

The court may accept the reasoning of the police as to what it was proportionate to do. (See *Plattform Artze für das Leben v. Austria* (1988) 13 EHRR 204, in regard to a protest for and against abortion. In this case, the police claim that they had applied the principle of proportionality in policing a demonstration was accepted.)

Strasbourg may, on the other hand, criticize the planning and preparation for an operation, as giving insufficient regard to human rights. (See *McCann v. the United Kingdom* (1995) 21 EHRR 97, a case about the use of lethal force in regard to a terrorist operation as referred to previously, but in which the same general principles apply as in policing a demonstration.) But the court's role, in general terms, is to bring the decision-making organization to account.

Freedom of association

Although this is a subject of very strong interest to both employer and employee, and a topic with a lengthy and bloody history, it has not generated a huge case history of complex and crucial decisions at Strasbourg. In essence, the right as stated is a simple one. People have the right to form and join trade unions at work for the protection of their interests, unless specifically exempted by the terms of the Convention itself. The armed forces, the police and members of the administration of the state, as the article states, may be subject to lawful impositions upon this right.

Who is a member of the administration of the state? That, presumably, is a matter to be raised in court by anyone who wishes to challenge a prohibition or restriction. GCHQ trade unionists in the UK objected to an infringement of their rights in this area when the government decided that they should no longer be unionized: but they were declared to be public officials and therefore subject to lawful restriction (*CCSU v. UK* (1987) 50 DR 228). Other appeals might succeed, for it is not necessarily the case that anyone who might be construed as working for the state could be subjected to the same restriction, for in the case in point there was an issue of national security.

Servants of the state such as police officers, members of the armed services and security officials may legitimately face some restrictions upon their rights and freedoms, we suppose, because those restrictions are necessary in protecting national security; because their role is vital in safeguarding the rights and freedoms of others; and because they have knowingly and voluntarily entered into a form of employment that imposes such restrictions.

Strasbourg has not looked kindly at appeals by national servicemen that their rights have been infringed during national service, although this was not something that they had chosen to do, and once again the principle of proportionality has been applied.

The weakest link in the security argument above is, in our opinion, the assumption that it may be necessary to impose a blanket restriction upon the freedom of expression of servants of the state, rather than their freedom of association. Here we are referring to the notoriously illiberal Official Secrets Act (1911), which was originally drafted in the most general of terms, and forbade those to whom it applied from discussing any aspect of their work with the press or other interested parties. In simple terms, everything was secret and nothing was permissible.

While this may have been administratively convenient for the state, it had both theoretical and practical disadvantages. The application of the Official Secrets Act has generated a number of highly controversial cases, and we wonder if the Act itself is compatible with the HRA. Certainly, the two Acts occupy different ideological territories, and it is not easy to reconcile their intentions.

Article 11 does not protect the closed shop – the compulsory unionization of a workforce either by the union itself, or for that matter by management on its behalf. To be compelled to join a trade union is an unacceptable infringement of a fundamental freedom, and its justification that compulsory membership achieves a collective benefit that could not otherwise be obtained, goes against the spirit of human rights.

Article 11 does not indicate what forms of industrial action are acceptable and what are not, and there is no explicit right to strike under ECHR. Case law refers to (some) national legal restrictions upon industrial action as being acceptable. It is significant that Article 11 combines the rights to freedom of association and assembly, and that ECHR confers no especial rights upon management.

CASE STUDIES

Gallery

A private art gallery in a quiet provincial town has mounted an exhibition of paintings that has aroused both admiration and hostility. That the paintings are of artistic merit is not disputed.

However, some people have found them to be both offensive and blasphemous, and the gallery owner is under pressure in some quarters to close down the exhibition and cease causing offence.

Needless to say, the exhibition is also being championed by other groups in the name of artistic freedom. The police have declined to intervene in this dispute as there has been no breach of the peace, and the gallery owner has been left to decide what to do. Both artistically and commercially, there is a strong case for remaining open, but she does not wish to offend local opinion unnecessarily.

What should she do?

Commentary

The gallery owner is a businesswoman and not the guardian of public morality. In any case, public opinion is divided – as the police have presumably recognized in their minimalist interpretation of their duties in this case. In our opinion the owner should continue to stage the exhibition, provided that its contents are not unlawful, and at the same time make every effort to avoid causing unnecessary offence, for example by warning visitors that some paintings may upset them, or by showing them under controlled conditions. The choice is then offered to potential viewers as to whether they wish to be offended or not. If any would-be censors remain dissatisfied, they may attempt a private prosecution for the offence of blasphemy – an unusual proceeding, but still a possibility.

Two further comments arise. Firstly, any restriction on artistic freedom, if it be needed at all, should be both limited and precise, with the object of addressing a proven and specific evil. Beauty, it has been said, is in the eye of the beholder, and so is evil. A picture of a child bathing may be an innocent and beautiful celebration of the joys of parenthood, or a stimulus to the lust of an irredeemable pederast.

Are we to remove the temptation because some will find it irresistible? As a general rule, we think not. The police need to address the crime of unlawful sexual intercourse and other crimes associated with pederasty by whatever means are most appropriate and least intrusive to the legitimate interests of others: and this does not include removing all possible incentives to offend. (On that logic, we might as well forbid the possession and display of expensive motorcars, lest someone face an overwhelming temptation to steal them!)

Secondly, it would be wise to establish a proven link between cause and effect before the state acts to remove an apparent cause. Do violent films promote violence on the streets, or not? This is a hotly disputed topic, and one on which informed opinion would appear to be divided. Under such circumstances we will remain on the fence and say that there is no obvious solution. It is essential, however, that a working democracy addresses such issues and reaches its decisions in full possession both of whatever research has been carried out and of the popular and minority view; and that it applies the logic of human rights in its reconciliation of the conflicting rights involved.

The war of Jenkins' hair

You run a private school, which has strict but fair regulations about appearance and behaviour. Your rules are made known to all pupils, prospective and actual, by means of your prospectus and other publications, and are prominently displayed in the school's corridors. Amongst other things, they insist that all pupils wear the school uniform as prescribed, do not wear jewellery, and do not dye their hair.

One morning you discover that Paul Jenkins, a boy of 14 with an indifferent record for attendance, attention and homework, has arrived at school having dyed his hair bright green, glued it into spikes, and inserted several rings in his nose and eyebrows.

An experienced head, you recognize that Paul is not unintelligent and has the potential to be a good scholar. However, he has some personal problems and your impression is that his parents have not provided the best of home environments for him. Whatever he asks for, he gets; and he has had no previous acquaintance with discipline, whether external or self-imposed.

After a quiet start at your school he is going through a rebellious phase, and what better to rebel against than a potentially unpopular regulation? It may even raise his esteem with the other pupils, upon whom he has so far made little impact.

Were he being educated at home, he could present himself as he liked, provided that his parents approved. However, he is your pupil, and his behaviour is clearly unacceptable. It is a clear breach of the rules, to which there is no exception. Moreover, if you were to allow this breach, it would be in defiance of your authority, and who knows to what that would lead? Rules are rules. They are there for the benefit of all, and Paul must accept them. He is suspended forthwith, with work to carry on with at home and instructions that he is to return his hair to its natural colour and shape and remove his facial jewellery before he will be allowed to return.

What are the possible human rights issues that might be raised in this case, and how might they be resolved?

Commentary

In principle, Paul or his parents could claim that he is being denied a right to freedom of expression; that he is being prevented from receiving education (First Protocol, Article 2); and that he is being discriminated against in regard to the above rights – if, for example, he could show that the same restrictions were not applied to other pupils. A litigious claimant might also raise other rights.

A private school is not a public authority. Therefore, it is not specifically obliged to act in accordance with human rights by the HRA. However, if these issues were raised in a court it would need to be able to defend its position. How might it do so? In brief, we would suggest the following arguments:

▌ The right to freedom of expression is a qualified one, and in this case has been legitimately and foreseeably restricted.

▌ Education is still available to Paul, who has denied himself of its advantages. If he persists in his behaviour, he could be educated elsewhere.

▨ There is no evidence of discrimination in the application of the school rules.

▨ The school may also wish to point out that its rules are based on a respect for welfare, or health and safety. For example, the wearing of facial jewellery in a school environment could be dangerous if other pupils sought to remove it. However, this may not be the path to go down. The school need not, in our opinion, set out to justify its rules, but point out that they were both known beforehand and fairly applied. By the same logic, the argument of precedent need not be raised. (The school does not need to argue that Paul's example could encourage misbehaviour by other pupils. It may be dealt with as a discrete issue.)

Finally, may we comment that here as elsewhere, Paul's case is probably better settled outside court than within. The school has possibilities for negotiation with the parents in question, and should be able to resolve this issue by non-legal and less expensive means.

Protest

Amongst its other business interests, Research Incorporated breeds animals for scientific research. Its activities are closely regulated and supervised by various government agencies and are the subject of the concentrated attention of various animal welfare groups such as the RSPCA, as well as other animal protest groups who believe in direct action. Over the past few years the organization's workforce has been subjected to sustained harassment and vilification, both at work and at home. The workforce is demoralized and production has declined.

Meanwhile, the police appear to be doing very little to help the company and its workforce, and have proved hostile to its own attempts to improve security, such as making more use of private security companies to carry out preventative patrols. Although the police cannot stop these patrols from operating, they have refused to supply any information to them, for example about known and dangerous activists – in contrast to their rather more informative attitude to Neighbourhood Watch schemes, which they officially support.

What are the human rights issues in this scenario?

Commentary

The activities of the company in question are perfectly lawful, as the HRA does not protect animals. At the same time, peaceful protest is permitted. If that protest is damaging the commercial interests of the company in question, then unfortunately for those concerned, the HRA does not obviously apply, since there is no right to go about one's business as such.

If, however, the activities of the protestors are damaging the rights of others, then that is another matter, and there are options open to the police or other public authorities in terms of restricting the right to protest and associated activities. In addition to the lawful restrictions offered to public authorities under 10.2 and 11.2, we would suppose that Article 1 of the First Protocol to ECHR is of possible relevance in that it states that every natural or legal person is entitled to the peaceful enjoyment of his possessions. Finally, a protestor who makes threats of violence against employees or anyone else is no longer a protestor but a person contemplating or committing crime, and the HRA does not protect that pastime.

Whether Research Incorporated creates its own security company or employs one already in existence, that security company must respect the rule of law. It is not, in our opinion, obliged to take positive measures to protect the right to protest. On the data that we have been given so far, Research Incorporated is not a public authority, and the fact that its activities have aroused public protest does not make it into one. Its security employees or subcontractors must confine their activities to lawful ones, but are entitled to concentrate upon protecting the company's interests.

May we add that the police have, of course, a positive obligation to protect employees against known threats to life (see

Osman v. UK (1999) I FLR 198, as discussed in Chapter 3), whatever private security measures may be employed. In addition, the right to protest is a qualified and not an absolute one, and although the police are obliged to uphold the right, it must not be practised at the expense of damaging the rights of others. ECHR was not passed for the benefit of single-issue fanatics, and the activities of at least some animal rights activists are wholly incompatible with the practices of a liberal democracy. Secrecy and terror are the tactics of the Nazis and not of peaceful protest.

Finally, it would be possible to examine from the point of view of human rights, any difference in approach taken by the police in regard to the type, quality or amount of information that they are prepared to supply to other groups. The police have a duty to prevent crime and to protect life and property. However, there are also issues of privacy and confidentiality, and some careful judgements will be needed here as to what may or may not be shared.

Blowing the whistle

The company in question, Secure Products, makes specialist communications equipment and other items for the security industry, and one of its main customers is the Ministry of Defence. Many of its products represent a large investment of specialist skill and knowledge, and their uniqueness is both of commercial value and of interest from the point of view of national security. All company employees are rigorously vetted on joining the company and closely supervised at work, and in addition sign confidentiality agreements so that they are not at liberty to discuss the details of their work either while in employment or for a certain period afterwards.

George Jackson, a highly qualified and respected electronics expert, is fired by the company for gross breaches of security and goes public on his grievances, thereby attracting media coverage. Amongst other things, he claims that Secure Products is unnecessarily secretive; that it creates and maintains an atmosphere of humiliation and fear at work; and that some of its products are being illegally sold to states with which it is officially forbidden to deal by the Foreign Office, with the connivance of the Ministry of Defence. In addition, he claims that it has suppressed information indicating that there is an increased level of cancer amongst operatives who have used some of its products for a period of a year or more. He intends to raise all these issues at the industrial tribunal at which he will be contesting his dismissal, and to couch his case in terms of human rights. He is particularly insistent upon his right to freedom of expression.

His estranged wife Isabel, also interviewed in the press, claims that her husband is talking nonsense and that there is no truth in his allegations. The reason why he was fired is because he had taken to drink and was incapable of functioning as a responsible scientist. The company was right to fire him and he deserves no sympathy.

Commentary

You will no doubt have passed on from this case, and be looking for something a little easier! In case you have not, here are some comments on this scenario from a human rights perspective.

Let us concentrate our minds by asking four questions:

1. Was George Jackson fairly or unfairly dismissed?

2. Are his allegations relevant or irrelevant to his dismissal?

3. Are they true or false?

4. What is the responsibility of the tribunal towards investigating them?

On the face of it, Mr Jackson may have been fairly dismissed if he made gross breaches of security for which this was the prescribed penalty. From the script it is unclear whether Mr Jackson's gross breaches of security were connected with his later allegations of impropriety or not, and this would need to be investigated. Even if they are *ex post facto* allegations, and not the cause of Mr Jackson's departure, they may need to be considered on their merits if the public interest is involved – which on the face of it sounds highly likely.

The Public Interest Disclosure Act (1998), which is intended to protect whistle-blowers, may be relevant, and the wise company is familiar with its provisions. (The really wise company will not act in such a way that the Act would be needed at all: but let us deal with the case as it is.)

The tribunal is a court, and therefore a public authority, and therefore responsible for upholding human rights. Mr Jackson will presumably carry out his intention of raising a large number of possible violations of human rights by Secure Products when he appears before the tribunal, and it must pay attention to these allegations.

It could be argued that Mr Jackson is not and will not be the victim of their consequences, such as an alleged increased risk of cancer, which will affect other people; and the tribunal is presumably entitled to concentrate upon its primary purpose.

Suppose the tribunal decides that some or all of Mr Jackson's allegations fall within its responsibility to investigate. With the possible exception of an allegation of a climate of fear, they are at least in principle statements of fact, and can be investigated as to their truth or falsity.

There are other issues here, which we leave to discussion or further research. This is our last case study, and we hope that it has achieved its purpose of bringing the text to life and allowing readers to apply its principles for themselves. Like the other cases, it does not deal with real people or episodes, and any reference that could be construed as applying to any real situation, organization or person is purely coincidental. Finally, the commentaries are intended as helpful, but neither exhaustive nor authoritative: and they cannot be relied upon to win a case!

10

Reflections

We have now completed the major purpose of this book, which is to offer a relatively brief and, we hope, readable guide to human rights, and to identify its salient features.

In addressing human rights we have restricted our coverage to what was necessary and have not explored every shallow, eddy and backwater of the main course of the river. Readers will not have found coverage of every right in the HRA, although most are included, and we have chosen to cover the issue of discrimination as does the Act itself, by weaving it into the text with other rights.

We hope that as a result of reading this book and pondering the cases posed therein, our readers will be better placed to assess past decisions, existing policies and future issues in the light of the broad principles of human rights. They will know what lawyers are talking about; they will have a clearer insight into any cases that they may have to research and address in depth; and they will be better placed to discuss the rights and wrongs of human rights in any context.

They will also have appreciated that the theory and application of human rights does not provide a complete solution to every problem. Human rights in themselves do not provide resources, such as extra hospital beds, more constables on the beat, or a better pupil/teacher ratio in schools. They do not turn the jobbing journalist into a high-minded guardian of the public interest, nor the politician into a statesman. They cannot always be easily reconciled with each other, as we have seen especially in the clash between the freedom of expression of the media and the right to privacy of the individual or family, and as can also be shown in many other clashes whether already realized or still potential.

Human rights doctrine is clearly of benefit in addressing such dilemmas. It provides a language and a method, which is in essence the application of the principle of proportionality writ large. But it does not thereby resolve dilemmas. People do that, in active and sometimes heated discussion; and that brings us on to our next point.

The values of the Council of Europe are the values of a liberal democracy. Whatever the issue that needs to be resolved, there is an underlying assumption that consensus is achievable and will be found. Active disagreement and protest are allowed, and indeed officially welcomed; but it must be non-violent and it cannot be destructive. Symbolic protest such as civil disobedience sits easily with the values of the Council of Europe. Direct action does not, and we are not sure of the place of passionate conviction within this consensual framework. Extremism does not recognize the virtues of proportionality, and radical change will never occur by consensus.

THE NEED FOR INFORMED CONSENT: A MEDICAL ANALOGY

The medical profession has redefined the relationship between the doctor and the patient. Benevolent paternalism is no longer in fashion, and the patient has a right to know not only what is wrong with him, but also what are the realistic chances of a cure. He needs to know enough to be able to give any proposed treatment his informed consent, reject it altogether, or seek alternative practices or practitioners. In other words, the patient needs to be able to participate on equal terms with the expert, in the process of the assessment of risk; for it is his health or life that is at stake.

There will be patients who are incapable of making decisions for themselves, and there will be occasions when the doctor will be right to withhold knowledge from the patient. But these will be proven exceptions to the rule. If the principle of informed consent is not applied, this must be the result of a proper appraisal of the situation at issue, rather than the bland application of some general formula. The presumption must be that the patient has the right to know, and the exception must be argued for by means of a process that would satisfy the objective observer that a real debate was taking place that could go either way.

INFORMED CONSENT: THE RIGHT OF ACCESS TO INFORMATION

Informed consent is the key, and the ability to make up his mind in full possession of the relevant facts is something that the ordinary citizen needs in his dealings with government in the same way as the patient in his dealings with the doctor, and with a greater justification. The notion of the parliamentary assembly that represents and thinks for the electorate – without having shared with that electorate the necessary information to make sensible and properly aware decisions – is unsustainable in the 21st century.

A successful democracy is an informed and challenging democracy. Information should not be doled out sparingly and only when it is asked for, so that like Oliver Twist we are made to feel that it is wrong to ask for more. Moreover, in the case of Oliver Twist he could at least see that there was more to give, whereas government will deny not only that the citizen should receive more of the information that he needs, but that there is in any case more information to offer, and will always reserve the right to veto access to information on its own terms.

From within the perspective of the official mind, we can understand the careful arguments that may be put forward to protect such parsimony. The official mind is instinctively cautious and obscurantist, whatever its party political hue, and is easily able to find reasons not only to deny something, but to conceal its existence in the first place. We need a change of both attitude and system to bring an end to the culture of secrecy and denial and to create an era of full citizenship, and the HRA is a means to that end.

If the UK is to develop as a real democracy and to overcome the cynicism of its electorate with regard to their elected representatives and appointed officials, then we believe that the right of access to information is an important addition to the country's charter of rights.

We are not disappointed that the Act (following ECHR) has largely ignored the so-called social and economic rights, leaving these to be achieved by other means, for those other means have proved effective. The UK has an impressive record in providing for the health, education, housing and welfare of its citizens, independently of any doctrine of human rights. The creation of a welfare state preceded the UK's involvement in the drafting of ECHR; and the state's wider responsibilities for social and economic well being of all citizens have long been accepted by all the major political parties.

However, the HRA will help the ordinary citizen to obtain his rights in some areas where the collectivist doctrine of the state may previously have failed him. If, for example, he is informed that in area A he cannot obtain treatment B that is freely or at least more easily available in area C, then he may have grounds for an investigation under human rights terms. Article 6 may be brought to apply, and the difference in treatment available between A and C will need to be justified. Health authorities may, of course, be able to produce very good reasons for the existence of differences of all kinds. Those differences, however, will need to be explicable in terms that can be reconciled with human rights.

In the same vein, the citizen who appeals against a planning decision that prevents him from building or extending the house of his dreams, may have a greater power at his disposal against the overwhelming powers of the state than existed hitherto. Strasbourg has, in fact, in general been cautious about planning appeals. It has remained well aware that most rights are qualified, that the state has important collectivist obligations, and that it would not be a fair balance of the rights of the individual and the community if anyone were able to build a house where he chose, supposing that he could buy the land. The state has every right to create a plan that husbands a scarce resource and works for the benefit of all, according to the normal democratic process.

However, the citizen does have a right to his day in court. If his appeal against a planning decision is heard, in effect, by the same body that is responsible for devising and applying the housing policy in the first place, then that is not a fair trial, because there is no effective right of appeal to an independent and impartial tribunal.

We cannot predict the future, and would be unwise to try. There are some constitutional issues that will only determine themselves in practice. We cannot yet know the long-term effects of the HRA upon the common law, the role of the judiciary, or parliamentary sovereignty itself; and it remains to be seen how judicial review will adapt and develop in order that human rights may be used as a sword as well as a shield.

The radicalism with which the new rights are applied will depend at least initially on the radicalism of the judiciary, and most of the indications so far are of caution. Indeed, the phrase in use at the moment is that both courts and tribunals are being 'robust about human rights'. Judges have struck down trivial or facetious appeals, and have shown themselves to be concerned not to debase the coinage of human rights. In some areas, conservative interpretations have been made, whereas in others there has been a more radical approach. But on the whole we accept what would appear to be the consensus of opinion of the experts, that the HRA has had a limited effect so far, and that the judges are likely to remain cautious.

The Court of Appeal has recently ruled upon the role of the Secretary of State in planning appeals in what might be called a conservative interpretation: ie, one that finds merits in the *status quo*. It has recognized the checks and balances already existing within our constitutional provisions against the arbitrary powers of the state, and sees no need to change the planning process as against the right to a fair trial.

At the same time, the right to privacy has been extended in a significant judgement arising from a dispute between rival magazines over the right to publish exclusive photographs of a fashionable wedding. From such unlikely sources does change emerge!

WHAT DOES ALL THIS MEAN FOR THE MANAGER?

We have addressed our text to the good manager, and pointed out just as he has a duty to respect and uphold human rights, so does he benefit from what they have to offer. *Rights Brought Home* (The Home Office, 1997) declares that the government's aim is to create a human rights culture in the UK.

We support that aim, with full recognition that rights and responsibilities go together. We do not see the HRA as the last adjustment of some carefully constructed edifice, whose main advantage it that it saves the cost and time of taking expensive claims to Strasbourg. This is a revolution, even if a very quiet one; and if we cannot predict all of the consequences of the Act in detail, we know that they will be far-reaching, both nationally and internationally.

We hope that this book will help its readers to consider some of those consequences, and in part to shape the future as well as to be shaped by it. The HRA allows the citizen to act for himself, where the lawyer or politician did not act for him: and it gives the manager the true right to manage, provided that his actions are consistent with human rights. But in the 21st century this will not be a static or passive undertaking. Management is about consensus, maintenance and support, and leadership is about challenge; the direction of a successful enterprise requires both.

11

Human Rights Act: the Articles in question

Article 2 – right to life

1. Everyone's right to life shall be protected by law. No one shall be deprived of his life intentionally save in the execution of a sentence of a court following his conviction of a crime for which this penalty is provided by law.

2. Deprivation of life shall not be regarded as inflicted in contravention of this Article when it results from the use of force which is no more than absolutely necessary:

   (a) in defence of any person from unlawful violence;

   (b) in order to effect a lawful arrest or to prevent the escape of a person lawfully detained;

   (c) in action lawfully taken for the purpose of quelling a riot or insurrection.

Article 3 – prohibition of torture

No one shall be subjected to torture or to inhuman or degrading treatment or punishment.

Article 4 – prohibition of slavery and forced labour

1. No one shall be held in slavery or servitude.

2. No one shall be required to perform forced or compulsory labour.

3. For the purpose of this Article the term 'forced or compulsory labour' shall not include:

   (a) any work required to be done in the ordinary course of detention imposed according to the provisions of Article 5 of this Convention or during conditional release from such detention;

   (b) any service of a military character or, in case of conscientious objectors in countries where they are recognised, service exacted instead of compulsory military service;

   (c) any service exacted in case of an emergency or calamity threatening the life or well-being of the community;

   (d) any work or service which forms part of normal civic obligations.

Article 5 – right to liberty and security

1. Everyone has the right to liberty and security of person. No one shall be deprived of his liberty save in the following cases and in accordance with a procedure prescribed by law:

(a) the lawful detention of a person after conviction by a competent court;

(b) the lawful arrest or detention of a person for non-compliance with the lawful order of a court or in order to secure the fulfilment of any obligation prescribed by law;

(c) the lawful arrest or detention of a person effected for the purpose of bringing him before the competent legal authority on reasonable suspicion of having committed an offence or when it is reasonably considered necessary to prevent his committing an offence or fleeing after having done so;

(d) the detention of a minor by lawful order for the purpose of educational supervision or his lawful detention for the purpose of bringing him before the competent legal authority;

(e) the lawful detention of persons for the prevention of the spreading of infectious diseases, of persons of unsound mind, alcoholics or drug addicts or vagrants;

(f) the lawful arrest or detention of a person to prevent his effecting an unauthorised entry into the country or of a person against whom action is being taken with a view to deportation or extradition.

2. Everyone who is arrested shall be informed promptly, in a language which he understands, of the reasons for his arrest and of any charge against him.

3. Everyone arrested or detained in accordance with the provisions of paragraph 1(c) of this Article shall be brought promptly before a judge or other officer authorised by law to exercise judicial power and shall be entitled to trial within a reasonable time or to release pending trial. Release may be conditioned by guarantees to appear for trial.

4. Everyone who is deprived of his liberty by arrest or detention shall be entitled to take proceedings by which the lawfulness of his detention shall be decided speedily by a court and his release ordered if the detention is not lawful.

5. Everyone who has been the victim of arrest or detention in contravention of the provisions of this Article shall have an enforceable right to compensation.

Article 6 – right to a fair trial

1. In the determination of his civil rights and obligations or of any criminal charge against him, everyone is entitled to a fair and public hearing within a reasonable time by an independent and impartial tribunal established by law. Judgement shall be pronounced publicly but the press and public may be excluded from all or part of the trial in the interest of morals, public order or national security in a democratic society, where the interests of juveniles or the protection of the private life of the parties so require, or to the extent strictly necessary in the opinion of the court in special circumstances where publicity would prejudice the interests of justice.

2. Everyone charged with a criminal offence shall be presumed innocent until proved guilty according to law.

3. Everyone charged with a criminal offence has the following minimum rights:

   (a) to be informed promptly, in a language which he understands and in detail, of the nature and cause of the accusation against him;

   (b) to have adequate time and facilities for the preparation of his defence;

   (c) to defend himself in person or through legal assistance of his own choosing or, if he has not sufficient means to pay for legal assistance, to be given it free when the interests of justice so require;

(d) to examine or have examined witnesses against him and to obtain the attendance and examination of witnesses on his behalf under the same conditions as witnesses against him;

(e) to have the free assistance of an interpreter if he cannot understand or speak the language used in court.

Article 7 – no punishment without law

1. No one shall be held guilty of any criminal offence on account of any act or omission which did not constitute a criminal offence under national or international law at the time when it was committed. Nor shall a heavier penalty be imposed than the one that was applicable at the time the criminal offence was committed.

2. This Article shall not prejudice the trial and punishment of any person for any act or omission which, at the time when it was committed, was criminal according to the general principles of law recognised by civilised nations.

Article 8 – right to respect for private and family life

1. Everyone has the right to respect for his private and family life, his home and his correspondence.

2. There shall be no interference by a public authority with the exercise of this right except such as is in accordance with the law and is necessary in a democratic society in the interests of national security, public safety or the economic well-being of the country, for the prevention of disorder or crime, for the protection of health or morals, or for the protection of the rights and freedoms of others.

Article 9 – freedom of thought, conscience and religion

1. Everyone has the right to freedom of thought, conscience and religion; this right includes freedom to change his religion or belief and freedom, either alone or in community with others and in public or private, to manifest his religion or belief, in worship, teaching, practice and observance.

2. Freedom to manifest one's religion or beliefs shall be subject only to such limitations as are prescribed by law and are necessary in a democratic society in the interests of public safety, for the protection of public order, health or morals, or for the protection of the rights and freedoms of others.

Article 10 – freedom of expression

1. Everyone has the right to freedom of expression. This right shall include freedom to hold opinions and to receive and impart information and ideas without interference by public authority and regardless of frontiers. This Article shall not prevent States from requiring the licensing of broadcasting, television or cinema enterprises.

2. The exercise of these freedoms, since it carries with it duties and responsibilities, may be subject to such formalities, conditions, restrictions or penalties as are prescribed by law and are necessary in a democratic society, in the interests of national security, territorial integrity or public safety, for the prevention of disorder or crime, for the protection of health or morals, for the protection of the reputation or rights of others, for preventing the disclosure of information received in confidence, or for maintaining the authority and impartiality of the judiciary.

Article 11 – freedom of assembly and association

1. Everyone has the right to freedom of peaceful assembly and to freedom of association with others, including the right to form and to join trade unions for the protection of his interests.

2. No restrictions shall be placed on the exercise of these rights other than such as are prescribed by law and are necessary in a democratic society in the interests of national security or public safety, for the prevention of disorder or crime, for the protection of health or morals or for the protection of the rights and freedoms of others.

This Article shall not prevent the imposition of lawful restrictions on the exercise of these rights by members of the armed forces, of the police or of the administration of the State.

Article 12 – right to marry

Men and women of marriageable age have the right to marry and to found a family, according to the national laws governing the exercise of this right.

Article 14 – prohibition of discrimination

The enjoyment of the rights and freedoms set forth in this Convention shall be secured without discrimination on any ground such as sex, race, colour, language, religion, political or other opinion, national or social origin, association with a national minority, property, birth or other status.

Article 16 – restrictions on political activity of aliens

Nothing in Articles 10, 11 and 14 shall be regarded as preventing the High Contracting Parties from imposing restrictions on the political activity of aliens.

Article 17 – prohibition of abuse of rights

Nothing in this Convention may be interpreted as implying for any State, group or person any right to engage in any activity or perform any act aimed at the destruction of any of the rights and freedoms set forth herein or at their limitation to a greater extent than is provided for in the Convention.

Article 18 – limitation on use of restrictions on rights

The restrictions permitted under this Convention to the said rights and freedoms shall not be applied for any purpose other than those for which they have been prescribed.

Part II. The First Protocol

Article 1 – protection of property

Every natural or legal person is entitled to the peaceful enjoyment of his possessions. No one shall be deprived of his possessions except in the public interest and subject to the conditions provided for by law and by the general principles of international law.

The preceding provisions shall not, however, in any way impair the right of a State to enforce such laws as it deems necessary to control the use of property in accordance with the general interest or to secure the payment of taxes or other contributions or penalties.

Article 2 – right to education

No person shall be denied the right to education. In the exercise of any functions which it assumes in relation to education and to teaching, the State shall respect the right of parents to ensure such education and teaching in conformity with their own religious and philosophical convictions.

Article 3 – right to free elections

The High Contracting Parties undertake to hold free elections at reasonable intervals by secret ballot, under conditions which will ensure the free expression of the opinion of the people in the choice of the legislature.

Part III. The Sixth Protocol

Article 1 – abolition of the death penalty

The death penalty shall be abolished. No one shall be condemned to such penalty or executed.

Article 2 – death penalty in time of war

A state may make provision in its law for the death penalty in respect of acts committed in time of war or imminent threat of war; such penalty shall be applied only in the instances laid down in the law and in accordance with its provisions. The State shall communicate to the Secretary General of the Council of Europe the relevant provisions of that law.

References

The Home Office (1997) *Rights Brought Home: The Human Rights Bill,* The Stationery Office, Norwich

Lerner, M (ed) (1961) 'On Liberty', in *Essential Works of John Stuart Mill,* Bantam Books, London

Magee, B (1973) 'The Open Society and its Enemies', in *Popper, Fontana Modern Masters,* Routledge and Kegan Paul, London

Starmer, K (1999) *European Human Rights Law,* LAG, London

Index

14624